# Contents

# Introductory note

The Yugoslav Revolution, the occupation of East Europe by the Soviet armed forces, and the profound social, economic, and political changes in that area following the Second World War presented some complex theoretical problems that challenged the capacities of Marxists for explanation. It required a prolonged and probing examination of the novel features of the shifting situation before clarification was achieved and a correct line worked out.

All the materials in this compilation, with the exception of the article by Tom Kerry, have been taken from the discussion in the Socialist Workers Party and in the Fourth International which took place around the question of the sociological nature of Yugoslavia and the countries of the "buffer zone" between the capitalist West and the Soviet Union. These varied contributions provide a profile of the different viewpoints in this controversy that eventually led to adopting the position that these countries should be designated as "deformed workers states."

The first article, "The Wohlforth Way: A Methodological Mutation!" by Tom Kerry, is reprinted here by way of introduction. This article was written in 1963 as part of a polemic against a small minority grouping in the Socialist Workers Party led by Tim Wohlforth (this group was soon to leave the SWP and form what was to become the "Workers League"). We have included this article for its concise summary of the evolution of the discussion on Eastern Europe within the Socialist Workers Party and the Fourth International.

NOVEMBER 1969

# THE WOHLFORTH WAY: A METHODOLOGICAL MUTATION!

By Tom Kerry

It was a foregone conclusion that the fallout from the methodological pyrotechnics of the Slaughter-Healy faction would produce some startling theoretical mutations among their offspring in the SWP. Not one to dally on the launching pad, Comrade Tim Wohlforth has gone into orbit with a novel variation of a concept that figured in the discussion on the class character of the East European states among all sections of the world Trotskyist movement in the period 1945–51: structural assimilation.

### A model discussion

The discussion on the evolution of the East European states, which concluded with the adoption in 1951 of the Third World Congress resolution on the "Class Nature of Eastern Europe," was one of the most fruitful and rewarding in our history. Comrades can learn a great deal from a study of that discussion. Conducted over a span of six years—the discussion on China, although an extension of the East Europe discussion, came later—the discussion was distinguished by its high theoretical level, the absence of factionalism and the virtual unanimous agreement reached at its conclusion.

It was a model discussion. It demonstrated the capacity of the Trotskyist movement to apply its collective thought through the process of democratic discussion and arrive at a correct solution to what was, admittedly, a new historical phenomenon of an exceedingly complicated character. I strongly urge the comrades to study the material of that discussion. Some of it is still available in discussion bulletins and some is scattered through the various issues of the magazine, *Fourth International,* covering the period in question. For an excellent historical outline of the development of the dispute I strongly recommend the report to the Third World Congress on the Evolution of Eastern Europe by Comrade Pierre Frank in the special 64-page issue of *Fourth International,* November–December, 1951.

### Search for factional club!

Unfortunately, in his perusal of the material, Comrade Wohlforth wasn't interested in learning—his sole concern was to search for a factional stick with which to beat Pablo over the head and, by association, the "Pabloite" SWP majority. To Wohlforth and his "co-thinkers," at home and abroad, "Pabloism" is synonymous with original sin. And one cannot be too choosy about one's methods in fighting the devil! In his anxiety to tweak the devil's tail, Wohlforth accords his "Satanic Majesty" credit where no credit is due.

The criteria established by the Trotskyist movement to define the class character of the state, according to Wohlforth, originated with Pablo and was smuggled into our movement in a typically sneaky and underhanded way, fooling everybody including Healy and Lambert. Everyone else, that is, except Wohlforth! He was taken in for a time, but no more, my friends, no more! Let's hear him out.

### Half theory or half theoretician?

In his "Cuban Way" document Wohlforth has a section which he entitles, with inimitable style, "On a Half Theory of the State." "We must turn briefly," he says, "to the party majority's theory of the nature of the Cuban state because, as we shall see, it is intimately linked with Pablo's new revi-

Reprinted from SWP *Discussion Bulletin,* Vol. 24, No. 17, May 1963.

sionist theory and cannot be logically separated from it. Joe Hansen states time and again in his lengthy 'Cuba—the Acid Test' that the party majority is simply utilizing the criteria for determining workers states developed in 1948 and applying it to Cuba today. This is a terrible oversimplification of what actually transpired in the highly important buffer state discussion held in our movement at the time." After this "brief turn," in the course of which Wohlforth disposes of Hansen's "oversimplification," he proceeds to give us the real score. Here it is:

"The *whole* truth is that the party majority today is utilizing a method for determining workers states *rejected* by the party majority at the February, 1950 plenum over the objections of Pablo, Cochran and Hansen at the time. Hansen is thus confusing his own *personal* political history with that of the party. The two have not always been identical.

"It was Michel Pablo," Wohlforth contends, "who first introduced into our international movement the now famous method of determining workers states by the simple procedure of finding out whether the basic industry is nationalized, the economy is under the direction of a planning commission, and there is a state monopoly of foreign trade. From the very beginning Pablo met strong resistance to this *method* of determining workers states from Germain and also from the majority of our party's National Committee. Some of the best comments on the essential method involved in Pablo's approach were made by the late John G. Wright and by Comrade Stein for the National Committee." (All emphasis in the original.)

### The Wohlforth school of history!

Such is party history a la Wohlforth. His perfervid loyalty to the "majority of our party's National Committee"—of 1950—is really touching. But has it ever occurred to Wohlforth that the 1950 N.C. majority might have been wrong and later corrected its position? Or did party history stop for Wohlforth with the February 1950 plenum?

Before I go any further, I want to state that Wohlforth's assertion that the decision of that plenum was taken over the "objections of Pablo" is pure fabrication. What were the actual sequence of events and the real, not fictionalized, positions of the comrades directly involved?

The dispute in the SWP over the class character of the buffer states broke out with the adoption of a resolution on the "Evolution of the Buffer Countries," at the April 1949 plenum of the International Executive Committee of the Fourth International—"Pablo's" IEC, as Wohlforth and Company keep insisting. It was published in the *International Information Bulletin* by the SWP under date of June 1949.

The resolution elaborated an analysis of the actual development in the buffer countries which was essentially correct in describing the transformations that had taken place since the outbreak of the "cold war" in 1946. However, the resolution stopped short of the logical conclusion of its analysis that these were "deformed" workers states. Yet the authors of the resolution felt compelled to take cognizance of the fact that the previous position adopted stating that these states were "capitalist states on the road to structural assimilation" with the Soviet Union, lacked precision and required amendment.

This the resolution attempted to do by qualifying the position previously held by the international movement as follows: "The social differences between the USSR and the buffer zone, enumerated above, are of a *qualitative* nature even though from the *quantitative* point of view society in the buffer zone approaches more closely Soviet society rather than that of 'normal' capitalist countries, in the same sense in which the USSR is quantitatively closer to capitalism than to socialism. Only in this sense can we continue to define the buffer countries as *capitalist countries on the road toward structural assimilation with the USSR*." (Emphasis in original.)

### Contradictory position challenged

The amendment was admittedly "awkward" and highly unsatisfactory. It resolved none of the contradictions in the position. This was the position supported by the SWP N.C. majority. In his report to the February 1950 plenum, Comrade Stein stated: "Our preliminary discussions in the Political Committee have revealed two positions: (1) that of the majority of the Political Committee which bases itself in general on the analysis and conclusions of the [2nd] World Congress theses and the IEC resolution [cited above]; and (2) that of the minority which considers that the buffer countries have ceased to be capitalist states and must now be considered as workers states (deformed or degenerated)." (*Discussion Bulletin*, No. 3, June 1950.)

The comrades who first challenged the position of the IEC-SWP majority were Joe Hansen and—to give another devil his due—Bert Cochran. (See: "Memorandum on Resolution on 'The Evolution of the Buffer Countries,'" by E.R. Frank (Cochran) in *Internal Bulletin*, Vol. XI, No. 5, October 1949. Also: "The Problem of Eastern Europe," by Joseph Hansen, Vol. XII, No. 2, February 1950 and "The Kremlin Satellite States in Eastern Europe, Yugoslavia, Marxist Theory and Our Perspective," by E.R. Frank, *Discussion Bulletin*, No. 1, April 1950.)

### The search for 'origins!'

If Wohlforth is seeking for the "origin" of our "three criteria" as he calls it, he will find it there and not in his own version of *Grimm's Fairy Tales*.

It's hard to make head or tail of what Wohlforth is after. For example, he now claims John G. Wright for his very own and strings together bits and pieces of quotations from Comrade Wright's article, which he presents as one continuous quotation, to prove that "his [Wright's] analysis is identical with the analysis we have made in our 'In Defense of a Revolutionary Perspective' and which the British have made in their writings on the basic method of the majority and the Pabloites."

Poor Usick! Those who knew and loved him can well imagine with what contempt and scorn he would have rejected Wohlforth's embrace. Comrade Wright never claimed to be infallible and was the first to admit an error when proven wrong. What is the point? In the article referred to, Comrade Wright endorsed the view that the buffer states were "degenerated capitalist states." Does Wohlforth now support that view? Presumably not. But, you see, he supports the "method" by which such a conclusion was reached. Just as he supports and extols the "method" of Slaughter-Healy, who conclude that: "On all decisive and fundamental questions which impinge upon the power and wealth of the national bourgeoisie as a whole, however, the [Cuban] regime comes down on the side of capitalism." Wohlforth supports the *method* but not the *conclusions* that are derived by the application of the method. Just as he supports the February 1950 majority but not the 1963 majority. Why? Is it his opinion that the 1950 majority was correct as against Hansen? Let's pursue the subject, however distasteful, a little further.

### Wohlforth sums up

After praising Comrade Stein for straightening Hansen out at the February 1950 plenum Wohlforth sums up:

"Thus we see Pablo's new *method* of determining workers states was repudiated by our party when it first appeared within our international movement because it was a false, *non-dialectical* method. In reality it was no theory of the state at all—it was a *half-theory* of the state, and interestingly enough the second half. As the comrades at the time noted, a real Marxist theory of the class nature of the state must *begin with* an analysis of the process which produced the resultant institutions existing in the state, like nationalized industry, state planning, etc. Obviously the nationalization of the coal industry by agents of the bourgeoisie in England is not the same thing as nationalization of the coal industry in Russia by agents of the revolutionary proletariat—and the difference is *more* than quantitative." How profound! How utterly profound! It just takes your breath away!

### It's all done with mirrors

Wohlforth too has *his* method. He quotes Stein against Hansen and with a quick flick of the wrist substitutes Pablo for Hansen in order to bolster his fictionalized version of party history. Isn't it amazing? Pablo's name isn't once mentioned in the whole of Comrade Stein's report. Stein is not one to resort to subterfuge in political polemics. The difference at that time between Pablo and Germain was over the Yugoslav development, not over the other buffer countries. Both supported the resolution of the 7th plenum of the IEC which was the position supported by Stein and the N.C. majority. So it could not have been "Pablo's new method of determining workers states" that "was repudiated by our party, etc., etc."

There was a change, however, in the basic position of "Pablo's" International Secretariat which was codified in resolution form for submission to the Third World Congress. The resolution was published by the SWP in its *International Informa-*

*tion Bulletin* of July, 1951. Entitled: "Draft Resolution on the Class Character of the European Countries in the Soviet Buffer Zone," it was adopted by the Third World Congress in 1951 and subsequently its line was approved by a convention of the SWP. It embodied the position of the party—and, I might add the world Trotskyist movement—on the class character of the buffer states. It was a confirmation of the correctness of the February, 1950 *minority* in the party. It is worth quoting at length, not only for the position it sets forth, but because it contains a key to the "new" Wohlforth theory of structural assimilation:

### Modified position of world movement

"Taking account of all the modifications effected since 1949 in the economy as well as in the state apparatus of the buffer zone countries, within the framework of a new international evolution, *it is necessary to state that the structural assimilation of these countries into the USSR has now become essentially accomplished and these countries have ceased to be basically capitalist countries.* (Emphasis in original.)

"The taking into tow of all these countries after the last war by the Soviet bureaucracy, the influence and decisive control it exercises over these countries, contained *the possibility* and even in the long run the *inevitability* of their structural assimilation into the USSR, by virtue of a certain relationship of forces at home and abroad, between the Soviet bureaucracy, the native bourgeoisie, imperialism and the masses.

"For a long period which by and large extended from 1945 to about 1948, the Soviet bureaucracy maintained these countries in an intermediate status of varying degrees because it was not yet ready to consider its break with imperialism as final and because of the necessity arising from its own nature of eliminating the native bourgeoisie by cold methods, without genuine revolutionary action by the masses over which it tried at the same time to impose a rigorous control.

"This intermediate status corresponded *sociologically* more and more to a regime of *dual power* both on the economic and the political planes, the economic structure remaining fundamentally capitalist. Beginning with 1949 this duality manifestly gave way to regimes which stabilized a structure essentially characterized by *property and productive relations* qualitatively assimilable to the USSR, that is to say, characteristic of an essentially *statized* and *planned* economy (except for the Soviet zone in Austria and Albania, where a regime of dual power still exists).

"Parallel with this process, the political power, which for a long time had been assumed by different combinations between the Stalinist leaderships and the representatives of the former bourgeois and petty-bourgeois parties, now passed exclusively into the hands of the Stalinists and was thus transformed in its form as well as in its social composition.

"The form of political power still remains marked by important differences from one country to another and in their entirety with that of the USSR, as is likewise the case so far as the form of political power in a capitalist regime is concerned. But it is above all by virtue of their economic base, of the structure essentially common to all the countries of the buffer zone, characterized by new *production and property relations belonging to a statized and planned economy, essentially like those of the USSR,* that we have to consider these states as now being *deformed workers states.*"

Since 1951 the above position, as elaborated in the resolution adopted by the Third World Congress, has been the methodology of the world Trotskyist movement.

It is the method we applied to our analysis of the Cuban state. But it was not until the unfolding of the Cuban events that we were confronted with a concerted attempt to alter or abandon our criteria and substitute for it the "dialectic" of the Slaughter-Lambert-Wohlforth faction. Slaughter-Healy have attacked our basic criteria without, however, substituting criteria of their own. The French have put a question mark over our criteria by announcing a "re-examination" of the whole buffer state discussion. But Wohlforth is not one to dally—he has plunged in, right over his head, and come up with his own criteria: "structural assimilation."

### Half-and-half jargon

Before proceeding to an examination of Wohlforth's latest brainstorm, let's finish with his "half-theory-of-the-state" hogwash. Wohlforth lays the foundation for his "half-theory" structure by falsifying party history in order to make it appear as though Pablo put over a package deal on the party and the international movement. In the Wohlforth schema there were two parts to "Pablo's" theory of the state. One, the "three criteria," constituted the "second half" and Pablo's theory of "centuries of deformed workers states" the first half.

"Pablo," he asserts, "in reality had a rounded theory of the creation of workers states which also accounted for the question of *origins*. His theory of 'centuries of deformed workers states' was logically and intimately connected with his theory of the state as a whole. He saw deformed workers states being created as a *general, universal* phenomenon, as a new stage for all proletarian revolutions for centuries."

With all due apologies to our latter-day theoretician he is mixing up two different things. One involves the criteria for determining the class character of a state in being, and the other a projection of an historical perspective of revolutionary development. Along with the entire world movement we arrived at a common agreement on criteria by the application of the methodology of Marxism. We rejected the perspective of "centuries of deformed" states, primarily because it excluded the perspective of the American revolution, a perspective which was codified in the line of the American Theses adopted by our 1946 convention. Now what did Machiavelli Pablo do to circumvent our opposition?

"This theory," Wohlforth informs us, "was so repugnant to our movement when it was first introduced that, in order to get it adopted, Pablo put forward the *second half* of his theory first and independent of the first half—that is his so-called 'three criteria.' This combined his political revisions in his 'centuries' theory with a methodological revision which has confused our cadres since. Hansen's 'Cuba—the Acid Test' is in reality nothing more than a 52-page compounding of this basic methodological error—it has no other content." A damn clever fellow, this Pablo, don't you think? But he's not pulling the wool over Wohlforth's eyes, no sir!

## For whom does Wohlforth speak?

"So, today," Wohlforth warns, "we face the same sort of situation. Pablo, and his supporters in our party (above all, Comrade Hansen once again) are once again putting forward the second half of their theory and demanding that one and all 'label' the Cuban state by means of their 'three criteria' first and discuss all other questions later. Well, we simply reject this *method* completely and refuse to recognize such a position as a *theory at all.*" And that's that!

Who is the "we" Wohlforth continually refers to? His new theory is presented presumably in his own name. Does it include the co-leader of his faction, Albert Phillips, together with his state capitalist position, as "reevaluated" and stashed away in his briefcase? We'll find out eventually, I suppose. In the meantime, having summarily disposed of Pablo and Hansen and their supporters, and having jettisoned our "three criteria" in the process, let's examine Wohlforth's double-barreled "dialectical" criteria for defining the class character of the state.

## 'Theory' of 'structural assimilation!'

Unlike Pablo, he lets us have both barrels at once. According to the Wohlforth theory there can only be two ways in which a workers state can be established. One, by the method of the classic revolutionary overturn exemplified by the Russian October, or, two, by "structural assimilation."

Wohlforth invests the concept "structural assimilation" with a meaning it has never had in our movement. From the way he applies it I gather he means structural assimilation in reverse. "The theory of structural assimilation," he says, "explained a *process* of the creation of deformed workers states through the *extension* of the degenerated workers state. That is it answered the question of origins without in any sense undermining the *revolutionary* role of the proletariat. This is especially the case if one realizes that the theory of structural assimilation sees this transformation taking place only in the *buffer regions* surrounding the USSR, and as a result of *defensive* steps taken by the Stalinist bureaucracy."

Because it is "defensive" it can only take place in geographical areas contiguous to the Soviet Union. That would rule out the process of structural assimilation for more remote areas like Algeria and Cuba—although, according to Wohlforth, in the case of Cuba it could apply only under exceptional circumstances. What he considers the vital question of "origins" I presume refers to the origin of the Soviet Union in a classic proletarian revolution which, though degenerated, still retained the basic economic conquests of the October Revolution.

### Ineluctable conclusion

If all of this is true, then we are confronted with the following equation—*Stalinism in power in any area bordering the Soviet Union equals structural assimilation equals workers state.* From our starting point of structural assimilation in reverse we arrive at the Marcyite theory of the "global class camp," although I must say the Marcyites had more justification for their "theory" that Stalinism in power equals workers state than does the Wohlforth theory.

It is a wholly schematic, anti-Marxist theory which has no basis in reality, either in the fact of the establishment of the buffer states nor in their subsequent evolution. The concept of structural assimilation had its origin in the dispute with the Shachtmanites in 1939–40. At one point in the discussion the Shachtmanite pundits characterized wartime Soviet expansionism as "imperialist exploitation."

### Trotskyist methodology

"Let us for a moment concede," argues Trotsky, "that in accordance with the treaty with Hitler, the Moscow government leaves untouched the rights of private property in the occupied areas and limits itself to 'control' after the fascist pattern. Such a concession would have a deep-going principled character and might become a starting point for a new chapter in the Soviet regime; and consequently a starting point for a new appraisal on our part of the nature of the Soviet state.

"It is more likely, however," Trotsky affirmed, "that in the territories *scheduled to become a part of the USSR,* the Moscow government will carry through the expropriation of the large landowners and statification of the means of production. This variant is most probable not because the bureaucracy remains true to the socialist program but because it is neither desirous or capable of sharing the power, and the privileges the latter entails, with the old ruling classes in the occupied territories. (My emphasis.)

"Here," added Trotsky, "an analogy literally offers itself. The first Bonaparte halted the revolution by means of a military dictatorship. However, when the French troops invaded Poland, Napoleon signed a decree: 'Serfdom is abolished.' This measure was dictated not by Napoleon's sympathies for the peasants, nor by democratic principles, but rather by the fact that the Bonapartist dictatorship based itself not on feudal, but on bourgeois property relations. Inasmuch as Stalin's Bonapartist dictatorship bases itself not on private but on state property, the invasion of Poland by the Red Army should, in the nature of the case, result in the abolition of private capitalist property, so as thus to bring the regime of the occupied territories into accord with the regime of the USSR." (*In Defense of Marxism,* New York, Pathfinder, 1942, 1995), pp. 68-69 [2012 printing].)

Implicit in this analysis of Trotsky's are the much maligned "three criteria" for determining the class character of the state. And thus it transpired with those territories *"scheduled to become part of the USSR."* Bits and pieces of real estate together with the three Baltic states, Latvia, Lithuania and Esthonia, were assimilated into the structure of the USSR. But Stalin pursued an altogether different course with the East European buffer countries at the close of the Second World War.

### The Stalin line

In the latter countries Stalin first used his military-bureaucratic power to install coalition governments in which representatives of the native bourgeoisie shared the political power with Stalin's hand-picked henchmen on the basis of the existing capitalist property relations. He followed a policy of pillage and plunder, exacting huge reparations, dismantling plant and equipment for shipment to the Soviet Union, setting up joint stock corporations to exploit the resources of the buffer zone countries, etc., etc. Obviously Stalin did not consider these territories *"scheduled to become part of the USSR."*

"Structural assimilation" was the furthest from his thoughts. This was indicated by the "peoples front" label applied to these countries which were designated "peoples democracies." With the launching of the cold war in 1946 and especially with the promulgation of the Marshall Plan for Europe, with Poland and Czechoslovakia making a bid for inclusion, Stalin recoiled in alarm. The order went out from Moscow—sharp turn to the left. The bourgeois ministers were unceremoniously booted out of office and there began the process of expropriating bourgeois property and transforming basic property relations.

### The process of evolution

At the beginning, the comrades in the world movement characterized these states as *capitalist* for the very obvious reason that capitalist property forms and property relations were left virtually intact. With the turn to the left, bringing in its wake the gradual transformation of all social relations and taking cognizance of the dual character of Stalinism, the comrades cautiously advanced the formula: "capitalist states on the road toward structural assimilation." This was more an inherent tendency than an actual fact. The *fact* of Stalin's determination was highlighted by the break with Tito.

The Yugoslavs, who occupied a more independent position in relation to the Kremlin because of the mass upsurge that led to the capture of power under the leadership of the native Stalinist cadre, sought to break out of the narrow national framework imposed by the Balkanized buffer countries. Each of the countries standing alone was completely dependent on the Kremlin for its economic existence. That was the way Stalin wanted it. When the Yugoslavs began advancing the idea of a Balkan-Danube federation Stalin reacted with savage ferocity. Tito was read out of the buffer zone family and unable to overcome his Stalinist background, failed to advance a revolutionary line, turning instead to western imperialism for economic aid.

A Stalinist purge swept the buffer states. This was Stalin's answer to anyone attempting to toy with the idea of federation. At the same time he barred the door to structural assimilation of the buffer countries. In retrospect, I believe that the "structural assimilation" concept was a fuzzy hypothesis employed to bridge the theoretical gap in the thinking of the SWP majority and the world movement. Our thinking lagged behind the development. This was not surprising considering the scope and complexity of the new phenomena under consideration. Instead of heaping opprobrium on the heads of those comrades who took the lead in prodding the movement toward a correct solution we should be grateful to them for their persistence in advancing their views in the discussion.

### Something 'new' has been added

But I repeat, *no one* during the whole course of the discussion ever conceived the idea of "structural assimilation" in reverse. That is Wohlforth's own unique contribution to the theory and practice of Marxism. Although Wohlforth's document is honeycombed with copious arguments borrowed freely from comrades on the wrong side of the buffer state dispute, reverse assimilation is his very own. Let's probe this concept a bit further.

The Bolsheviks viewed the October Revolution as the beginning of the European and world revolution. The program called for the establishment of the Socialist United States of Europe as the prelude to the world revolution. In line with this view they designated the first workers state as the *Union of Soviet Socialist Republics.* The extension of the revolution, especially to one of the advanced capitalist states, would bring powerful economic and political reinforcement through "structural assimilation" based on division of labor under one integrated master plan. That was the programmatic norm of Bolshevism. Historical development proved to be much more complex.

With the victory of Stalinism, the basic policy of the bureaucratic caste was summed up in the theory of building socialism in a single country. This meant subordinating the interests of the world revolution to the fantasy of carving out of the capitalist world a "socialist" utopia in one country. It was from the basic standpoint of building socialism in the Soviet Union that Stalin approached the territorial conquests of World War II. The buffer states were plundered and bled to begin again the process of "building socialism" in the USSR. When Stalin was forced to execute his left turn he did so without any thought of abandoning his basic policy. While the exigencies of the cold war compelled some degree of economic integration and joint planning, it was at the expense of the economic development in the buffer states.

### Criteria projected by Germain

Each of the Balkanized buffer states elaborated its own "plan." It was precisely this aspect of the problem that Germain focused attention on in his article in the September 1949 *Fourth International* entitled, "Whither Eastern Europe: Economic Trends in Stalin's Buffer Zone." Germain took as his point of departure the hopelessness of "socialist planning" on the basis of these atomized states.

"Economic planning," he pointed out, "requires not only nationalization of all means of production and exchange (of which the land remains the most important element in agricultural countries). It also requires the abolition of national frontiers which, along with the private ownership of the means of production, constitutes an absolute brake on any growth of the productive forces. This is not only a Marxist axiom, a general and abstract point of view opposed to the absurd theory of 'socialism in one country.' It is also an absolutely basic consideration for the purpose of defining the character and possibility of a given economy. Construction of a socialist economy is possible only on an international plane. With the exception of a few ultralefts, no one in the communist wing of the movement has ever disputed the possibility of *making a start* in this construction during a transitional period within that concrete national framework established by the victory of the proletarian revolution.

"It was the Left Opposition itself which, toward this end, drafted the first plan in the USSR against the violent resistance of the bureaucracy and of the Stalinist faction. But, it does not at all follow from this that *any* national framework whatever lends itself to planning on the mere condition that the proletariat had conquered power. It is obvious that a *minimum material base* is indispensable even to the preparatory work of socialist planning. To *make a start* to the building of socialism in Rumania, in Luxembourg or in Paraguay is an even more patent absurdity than to pretend that this construction is *being completed* in the USSR."

## The I.S. modifies stand

These were cogent arguments. But they did not stand up in the discussion. Germain was compelled to abandon "socialist planning" and the "abolition of national frontiers" as criteria in the determination of the class character of the buffer states. It was this concept, I believe, that led, first to the formula of "capitalist states on the road toward structural assimilation," and then later to the erroneous conclusion of the I.S. Draft Resolution submitted to the Third World Congress which asserted:

"Taking account of all the modifications effected since 1949 in the economy as well as in the state apparatus of the buffer zone countries, within the framework of a new international evolution, *it is necessary to state that the structural assimilation of these [buffer] countries into the USSR has now become essentially accomplished and these countries have ceased to be basically capitalist countries.*"

Recognizing the obvious contradiction between theory and fact, the resolution did add: "It has turned out on the other hand that in the same conditions and on the basis of an effective statization of the means of production, it is possible to initiate the process of a planned economy without formal incorporation into the USSR, without formal abolition of the frontiers and despite the special forms of exploitation that the bureaucracy still maintains in these countries and which remains an ever-present obstacle to the planning and free development of their country."

Even a cursory examination of the buffer zone discussion material should make it obvious to all but the factionally blind that the formula "structural assimilation" meant incorporation within the structure of the USSR under a single integrated economic plan. While the "tendency toward structural assimilation" holds true in the historic sense, the fact is that the process has not been completed—far from it—even though some halting steps toward integrated economic planning have taken place with a limited number of the buffer states through Comecon (Council for Mutual Economic Aid)—the Soviet counterpart to the European Economic Community and the Common Market.

## Some pertinent questions

But *is it true of Yugoslavia,* whose economy is more "integrated" with the west than with the east? *Is it true of China,* which from the beginning has had its "own" economic plan and today has been cut off from all significant Soviet economic aid? And *what of Albania,* which has been entirely cut off from Soviet economic aid and with whom Moscow has even broken diplomatic relations? Are these still to be considered "workers states" under the new Wohlforth dispensation of reverse structural assimilation? If so, on the basis of what criteria? We shall see when we come to Wohlforth's application of his theory to the question of Cuba.

### Cuba—the acid test!

Here the Wohlforth theory is revealed in all its glory. Cuba again provides the "acid test"!

"Thus we see that the process which has been going on in Cuba," says Wohlforth, "differs radically from the process which transformed the buffer areas into deformed workers states. The erosion of the former capitalist state apparatus, the destruction of the internal power of the national bourgeoisie, the swing from the international capitalist orbit—all these events had occurred in Cuba just as they have occurred in the buffer areas. But the *consummation* of this process through the creation of a monolithic *Stalinist* party and the *fusion* of this party with the state apparatus has not taken place nor is it likely to take place in the near future. Thus Cuba is more like these states before the structural process was completed—that is like Eastern Europe between 1947–49 and China between 1949 and 1953."

### The circle is squared!

Now if this means anything at all, it means that there is just one ingredient lacking for Cuba to earn the right to be designated a workers state and that is—Stalinism in power! Here we have Wohlforth's "criteria" in all its pristine purity.

To remove all question about what Wohlforth means he elaborates for us on this theme. "The situation in Cuba by late 1961 and early 1962," he says, "had reached a point where it *appeared* as if the country was going through the same structural assimilationist process as did Eastern Europe and China. Nationalizations had been carried through, the national bourgeoisie was pretty much routed from the country, economic ties with the Soviet bloc were extremely close, and in addition Stalinism seemed to be on the march throughout Cuba. It seemed as if it would be only a short time before the completion of a formation of a Stalinist type party and the subordination of the state apparatus to this party would be evident. Some of the minority comrades, reacting to this *appearance* of reality, declared Cuba to be a deformed workers state at that time."

### Caught off base

Presumably these "minority comrades" have now reversed their position. If, instead of purging Escalante, Castro had been purged by the Stalinists, then the "minority comrades" would have bestowed upon Cuba the accolade of "deformed workers state." Shouldn't we then have ranged ourselves on the side of Escalantism against Castroism? I know that the British are much disturbed about Escalante being deprived of his "democratic rights," but I never dreamed it had gone this far!

Wohlforth goes to great pains to point out where some of his "minority comrades" went off base. In the process he renders the confusion worse confounded. "The Escalante Affair," he says, "was soon to show that this was a superficial analysis of the processes going on in Cuba. This was not only because the Stalinists failed to consummate their control of the Cuban state apparatus but also because of a misunderstanding as to the *political role* of Stalinism within Cuba. It is a great mistake to identify Stalinist influence within a state as automatically meaning the structural assimilation of that state. *While this turned out to be the case in Eastern Europe and China* (my emphasis!!!) the role of Stalinism in Spain was quite different."

So . . . while Stalinist influence in Eastern Europe and China "automatically" meant "structural assimilation" of those states it does not "automatically" follow that such would be the case in Cuba—where they follow the Spanish pattern. How can anyone make sense out of this drivel? The Stalinists in Spain, says Wohlforth, were not interested in "structural assimilation" so they used their "considerable control" to prop up the capitalist system, crush the revolutionary forces, murdering thousands of militants in the process, in the name of peoples frontism and peaceful coexistence with world imperialism.

### Doing the Wohlforth twist

But, Comrade Wohlforth, if I understand the whole thrust of your argument, based on your "two criteria," there can be no such thing as "structural assimilation" for areas remote from the borders of the Soviet Union. Cuba is ruled out and is placed in the same category as Spain in the 1930's and Algeria today. Therefore, Stalinism in power in Cuba, following the Spanish example, would lead, not to "structural assimilation" or the establishment of a "deformed workers state," but to the crushing of the revolution and the reestablishment of capitalist property forms and property relations. But this would mean the end of Stalinism in Cuba even if—I should say especially if—they succeeded in carrying through such a counterrevolution.

Do you really believe that the Kremlin, even in its maddest moments, would or could countenance such a role for their agents in Cuba? And if they tried it, what do you think the reaction would be in Latin America and China, not to speak of the rest of the world—including the masses in the Soviet Union itself? Cuba is not Spain. And we live in the year 1963 not 1936–37 when the Soviet Union was isolated after the defeat of the Chinese revolution in 1927, the victories of fascism in Europe, etc., etc. Wohlforth seems to be playing around with some new concept of Stalinism which imparts an infantile fuzziness to all of the ideas which he tries to pass off as some new and unique contribution to Marxist theory.

### Something 'new' in sociology

Aside from the question of criteria for the determination of the class character of the state, Wohlforth offers something "new" in the realm of "Marxist" sociology that defies understanding.

### Again—the imperial 'we'!

Wohlforth is notably lacking in one trait—a sense of modesty. In his approach to the "class character of the Cuban state," he avers that *his* is the exact methodological approach used in "Trotsky's pioneering work on the USSR." And here it is:

"We," Wohlforth declares, "will approach the process going on in Cuba in the same method (as that of Trotsky, T.K.) noting of course that here we are studying a revolutionary rather than a counterrevolutionary process. Thus the movement of the process is in an opposite direction though its *motion* must be understood with a common Marxist method. The Cuban Revolution had in its first stage a *capitalist* apparatus, weakened, yes, but still capitalist. All agree to this. This state apparatus has undergone a deep process of erosion under the impact of profound *revolutionary* developments. So profound has this process been that Cuba today certainly *looks* as if it were a workers state. But has the Cuban state changed *qualitatively* during this period? No, our study reveals profound social and political changes but no qualitative change either by the method of the transformations of the buffer nor by the method of October itself. (Wohlforth's two criteria! T.K.) Thus we must characterize this state as a *decomposed, partially eroded* capitalist state susceptible to the pressure of the working class as well as other social forces but not under the control directly or indirectly of the working class (or as the French have characterized it 'un etat bourgeois, delabre, decompos, fantomatique'). By the way of analogy we would say that the Cuban state has the same essential class character as the East European states between 1947–1949 and the Chinese state between 1949–52."

### Our modern-day Thor

Then Wohlforth hurls his challenging thunderbolt: "Those who consider such a designation as 'revisionist' or absurd had better tell us first how they would characterize the East European and Chinese states *during* the period in which they were being transformed into deformed workers states."

Wohlforth imagines he is the first to pose that question. It was posed and answered, not once, but many times during the whole course of the discussion of the buffer states. It was answered, for example, in the section of the I.S. Draft Resolution submitted to the Third World Congress, cited in the early part of this article. Briefly, before they carried through their basic social transformations, the buffer states and China were characterized as regimes of dual power, unstable, temporary and transitional, based upon an "economic structure remaining fundamentally capitalist." In our view they became deformed workers states when they carried out a fundamental change in the previously existing capitalist property forms and capitalist property relations.

Cuba also went through a stage of dual power which was terminated with the ousting of Urrutia and the expropriations of capitalist property in the fundamental sectors of the economy, followed by nationalization, economic planning and the monopoly of foreign trade. Does Wohlforth contend that a dual power regime exists today in

Cuba? And if it does upon what property forms is it based?

Wohlforth has a little explaining to do about how he arrives at the bizarre conclusion that Cuba today is analogous to the East European buffer states of 1947–49 and the Chinese state between 1949–52. He has already informed us that in China and the buffer countries "Stalinist influence" had "automatically" meant "structural assimilation." But Stalinist influence in those states was very much present prior to 1947 in the buffer zone and prior to 1952 in China. What has happened to the "automatic" conversion theory? It seems Wohlforth forgets, between one paragraph and another, not only what he has said but what in the blazes he is driving at!

### Acrobatic display of ignorance

Wohlforth's display of ignorance of Marxist theory is astounding. He speaks of the Cuban "state apparatus" which has "undergone a deep process of erosion, etc." Then, he adds, "so profound has this process been that Cuba today certainly *looks"* like a workers state. He constantly confuses basic economic structure with political superstructure. The "state apparatus" can apply only to the regime, the administrative apparatus, the government. How can a "deep process of erosion" in the state apparatus make Cuba *look* like a workers state?

You never know what he's talking about. For he follows this profound observation with the assertion that no qualitative change has taken place in the Cuban state. Is he referring to the "state apparatus" or the statized economy? He's wrong, of course, on both counts.

### Methodology of a trapeze artist

Just one more joust with Wohlforth's sociology before I conclude. "Castro," he says, "today remains partially independent of the Kremlin but the Kremlin also exerts pressure on Castro through the complete dependence of the Cuban economy on the USSR. Castro partially 'aceeds' (sic) to this pressure as well. Castro does not represent the rule of Stalinism in Cuba, nor does he represent the rule of the peasantry, nor we are sad to say does he represent the rule of the working class. The state apparatus remains independent of the direct control of any of *these three major social forces* in Cuba today and under the direct influence of *all three forces*. (My emphasis, T.K.) In fact, the Castro regime plays an essentially Bonapartist role balancing between these forces and their international allies seeking all the time to maintain its independence from all."

How about a little of that Trotsky methodology, Comrade Wohlforth? Earlier in this article I cited Trotsky's reply to the Shachtmanites in which he took up the question of Bonapartism. What property forms and property relations does "Bonaparte" Castro defend? Upon what social foundations does his "Bonapartism" rest? Wohlforth advances his "three major social forces" as the tripod upon which Castro is "independently" perched. It is a basic tenet of Marxism that there can be no fundamental social transformation unless the means by which capitalist exploitation exist are radically altered. The nationalization of the means of production and exchange issuing out of a social revolution completely transforms the basic property forms and property relations. This is the basic foundation, without which there can be no talk of socialism. This is what we mean when we speak of economic structure. It is from this basic principle that we derive our criteria for the determination of the class character of the state.

Wohlforth abandons this basic Marxist approach by seeking constantly for his criteria in the superstructure. Thus he has Castro suspended in midair with no visible means of social support. Some trick if you can do it!

Having been deprived of their means of exploitation the bourgeoisie, as a class, has disappeared in Cuba—by Wohlforth's own admission. As a substitute we have "Stalinism." But not Stalinism of the Cuban variety. That could scarcely be considered any kind of a "force" in Cuba. No, Stalinism in the form of the Kremlin upon whom the "Cuban economy" is completely dependent.

So we have the following theoretical conclusion: Castro is a "Bonaparte" independent of the "direct or indirect" control of the workers and peasants of Cuba, and completely dependent on the Kremlin to survive. Doesn't that make Castro a pawn of the Moscow bureaucracy and Cuba therefore eligible for the title of a "structurally assimilated deformed workers state"? Make sense of it those who can!

Trying to grapple with Wohlforth's theoretical lucubrations is like trying to wrestle a greased eel!

**In conclusion**

I want to conclude by taking up the note upon which Wohlforth ends his document. "Pabloism," Wohlforth declares, "is the abandonment of *proletarian revolution itself* and that is the long and short of it. The deep crisis now going on within the Pabloite ranks is but a reflection of the instability of a petty-bourgeois formation which has abandoned the working class for a 'middle course.' The division between Trotskyism and Pabloism is thus clearly a *class* division. This division cannot be bridged; it can only be deepened. The international cadres of Trotskyism can only be reassembled, strengthened, rebuilt, around a *proletarian* line. There is no 'middle course.'"

In line with the "method" of the Slaughter-Healy faction, now so deftly applied by our own minority, the SWP has "capitulated" to "Pabloism" as defined in the purple prose of Wohlforth cited above. If you mean what you say, Comrade Wohlforth, we find ourselves on opposite sides of the barricades, divided by an unbridgeable gulf. Are we to understand your implied threat as an "either/or" declaration of intent? You might as well know right now that we cannot be intimidated into changing a course we consider correct and necessary. We have heard that kind of talk before. It hasn't fazed us a bit. Others have tried it before you—to no avail. Whether you stay with the party or take your departure for parts unknown is a matter which cannot influence us one bit. The door swings both ways—the decision is yours!

# THE EVOLUTION OF THE BUFFER COUNTRIES

## *Resolution of the Seventh Plenum of the International Executive Committee of the Fourth International, April 1949*

1. Important changes have taken place in Eastern Europe during the year 1948. The nationalization of industry, of the banking system, of communications and transport, have been practically completed in Bulgaria, in Yugoslavia, and in Czechoslovakia; it is on the road to completion in Poland and in Hungary, and it has had a big start in Rumania. Wholesale trade is equally on the road to statification in most of these countries. Only retail trade and agriculture remain as yet largely in the hands of private proprietors. The development of the cooperative system in these two spheres has been more and more removed from the influence of bourgeois elements following increased state intervention, but it continues to operate within the framework of small capitalist production. Finally, foreign trade, which is carried on mostly by state firms, continues to depend largely on relations with the so-called Western countries, among which Great Britain tends to substitute for the United States as the most important supplier and customer. This applies particularly to the more advanced buffer countries (Poland, Czechoslovakia, Hungary). The development of Finland and the Soviet-occupied zones of Germany and Austria, which are also part of the "strategic buffer" of the USSR, has nevertheless been profoundly different from that of the other buffer countries, and must be treated separately.

2. To the economic changes mentioned above correspond a whole series of political and ideological changes which are very significant. The last political opposition parties have been eliminated in all these countries (once more excepting Finland and the occupied zones of Germany and Austria, with their separate development). The liquidation of the independent Social Democracy has been concluded with the fusion of the PPS and the PPR in Poland. The last few months have been marked by an attack against all the churches independent of the state, the only remaining centers of a potential rallying of the political opposition. The totalitarianization of social life has been complete, depriving in the first place the proletariat, the only class which has retained a minimum of social cohesion in these countries in the process of transformation, of all possibility of expression for its cares and interests. At the same time the Stalinist party has made an ideological turn. While in the past the buffer countries were characterized as transitional between "capitalism" and "socialism" they now characterize the states as well as the economy of these countries as "socialist." This ideological turn has been consummated by the new thesis which identifies the regime of the "popular democracy" with the "dictatorship of the proletariat," in flagrant contradiction to all the past affirmations.

At the same time, the social contradictions, violently suppressed by the Stalinist dictatorship, have begun to express themselves even inside the Stalinist parties, thus creating the most serious dangers both for the monolithic system of international Stalinism (relations with the Kremlin) as well as for that of the different Stalinist parties in the buffer countries. The absolutist and bureaucratic methods, as well as the fundamental orientation of the Soviet bureaucracy, trampling upon the most immediate interests of the masses and of the economy of the buffer zone to its own advantage, have provoked such a tension inside the Stalinist apparatus itself, that the Kremlin has been forced to resort to preventive action (Tito) or to terrorism

Reprinted from *International Information Bulletin*, June 1949.

against the leading elements of the buffer zone apparatus (Koce, Kostov).

This crisis of Stalinism must inevitably extend and deepen inasmuch as the economic, social and national contradictions in the buffer zone are sharpened and as the Kremlin attempts to impose everywhere its absolute and direct control over the Communist Parties.

### I. The stages in the evolution of the buffer countries

3. As indicated in the theses on the *USSR and Stalinism* adopted by the Second World Congress of the Fourth International, the particular situation of the buffer countries resulted from a series of particular historical developments in these countries.

a. The enfeeblement (Finland, Rumania, Hungary, Bulgaria) or the virtual disappearance (Poland, Yugoslavia, Czechoslovakia) of the former possessing classes and the collapse of their state apparatus during the war, the military defeats, the Nazi occupation, the guerrilla wars, the Russian occupation, etc.

b. The decisive economic, political and military weight attained by the USSR in these countries following its military victories.

c. The revolutionary upsurge which developed in some of these countries parallel with the conclusion of the war (Yugoslavia, Poland, Czechoslovakia, Bulgaria).

d. The canalization (Yugoslavia, Bulgaria) or the strangulation (Poland, Czechoslovakia) of this upsurge by the Russian army or by the native Stalinist parties or by a combination of the two.

The decisive factor which permitted the evolution of the buffer countries to be what it was, was the non-intervention of the imperialists in these countries, who practically abandoned their extremely weakened bourgeoisie to the crushing political and military superiority of the Stalinist bureaucracy. Only this non-intervention explains why the resistance of the dying propertied classes in these countries could up to now be liquidated step by step by the Stalinists through "cold" means, without any broad mobilization of the masses being required. But this non-intervention of the imperialists is in turn a result of a definite historical conjuncture:

a. From 1944 to 1946 it corresponded to the accords of Teheran, Yalta and Potsdam, and constituted the price which world imperialism paid Stalin for crushing the German proletariat and for his active aid in strangling the insurgent Greek and Italian movements as well as for his aid in the reconstruction of the capitalist states and economies of all the countries on the continent outside the buffer countries.

b. From 1947 to 1949, it corresponded to the relationship of military and political forces in the "cold war" as it appeared on the European continent, that is, especially to the crushing superiority of the Russian army over all the other armed forces in Europe, to the permanent instability of the capitalist regime outside the buffer countries (strikes and constant disturbances, etc.), which made completely illusory and materially impossible any direct intervention in favor of the disappearing bourgeoisie of the buffer zone.

4. In the framework of this concrete historical conjuncture, the policy of the Soviet bureaucracy and of the Stalinist parties in the buffer countries likewise passes through two distinct stages:

a. The first stage which lasted up to the end of 1947, during which the Stalinist bureaucracy sought above all an empirical solution to the *immediate problems*. During this period, the accent of this policy was placed on the utilization of the resources of the buffer countries in order to attenuate as much as possible the effects of the reconversion crisis in the USSR itself. This is why, on the one hand, a whole series of measures were carried out for the exploitation of these countries for the profit of the Soviet bureaucracy (armistice agreements, treaties, reparations, seizure of the former German properties, mixed corporations, commercial treaties with preferential tariffs, etc.). And, on the other hand, each one of these countries was more or less left to itself as far as its own immediate problems of economic reconstruction are concerned. During this period, the bourgeoisie generally retained strong economic positions, if not predominant ones, in all these countries with the exception of Yugoslavia. The nationalizations were limited to enterprises seized by the workers at the end of the war, and which remained without legal proprietors. This stage can be characterized as an effort by the Stalinist bureaucracy and the native Stalinist parties to utilize the capitalist production relations for their own profits.

b. The second stage commenced when the Stalinist ban on the participation of these countries in the Marshall Plan took form, but developed more fully only at the beginning of 1948. During this stage, which incidentally marked the solution of the most dangerous immediate problems for post-war Soviet economy, the policy of the Soviet bureaucracy in the buffer zone consisted essentially of consolidating its predominant position in these countries on a long-term basis, counteracting the efforts of American imperialism to push it back into its own orbit. Within the framework of this new orientation of the Soviet bureaucracy are included, above all: The liquidation of the strong positions of the native bourgeoisie in industry and commerce; the initiation of an effort for the economic development and industrialization of these countries in a "planned" manner; the limitation of the Kulaks' grip on agriculture. Nevertheless, this new orientation of the Soviet bureaucracy could not eliminate from the economies of the buffer countries the structural difficulties of planning, which resulted from the Stalinist policy in the previous stage: The existence of a Soviet mortgage on the economies of these countries; the narrow national limits in which they remain enclosed; the capitalist character of agriculture; the apathy and often the passive hostility of the proletariat towards the bureaucratic "planning" efforts, etc. This is why "planning" retains its hybrid character and differs as yet structurally, in a fundamental way, from Soviet planning, which is itself the bureaucratic deformation of real socialist planning.

These variations in the politics of the bureaucracy do not correspond only to changes in the objective situation. Bureaucratic empiricism reflects, under the mask of immediate worries, the absence of historical perspectives and the impossibility of adopting a fundamental orientation. This in turn corresponds to the concrete relationship between the bureaucracy, the bourgeoisie, and the proletariat. Because it wanted first of all to strangle all possibility of a proletarian revolution, it was led to conclude a temporary compromise with the bourgeoisie; because its privileges are historically incompatible with the maintenance of the capitalist regime, it had to take the course of gradual and bureaucratic "liquidation" of the capitalist forces in the buffer zone.

5. Just as in the first stage the Soviet bureaucracy was led to conclude empirically that a step-by-step integration of the buffer countries with its own economic system is impossible as long as a sizeable economic power of the native bourgeoisie remains, so the bureaucracy is now beginning to understand from its sad experiences every day, that this same kind of integration remains impossible without eliminating the structural barriers which the bureaucracy itself put up against all genuine planning in the economies of these countries.

The experience of the Tito split has served as an example of the danger of the Stalinist parties in power in the buffer countries becoming the transmission agents of the contradictory social forces which develop as a consequence of the growing economic difficulties. The danger of growing imperialist pressure with the conclusion of the first stage of the Marshall Plan, the relative recovery of Western German industry, American rearmament, etc. have had the same effect. Thus a third stage in the evolution of Stalinist policy towards the buffer countries takes form. This is characterized up to now by the following signs:

a. Measures of growing economic coordination between the different countries, measures which have culminated in the constitution of a Council of Mutual Aid and which appear to develop in the direction of a pool of available resources for exports and of a Customs Union.

b. The first measures to abolish or lighten the Russian mortgage on the economy of these countries (sale to Bulgaria of German goods seized by the USSR in 1944; reduction of Hungarian, Rumanian and Bulgarian reparations; granting of gold and currency credits to Poland and Czechoslovakia, etc.).

These measures only indicate the possibility of a new stage of Stalinist policy in relation to the buffer countries, however, and cannot by themselves, or by means of the plans outlined up to the present and which are scheduled up to 1952, modify fundamentally the structural obstacles to "planning" in the buffer zone, even within the limits of Soviet planning.

## II. The social nature of the buffer countries

6. From the foregoing, it can be deduced that the buffer countries—aside from Finland and the Soviet-occupied zones in Germany and Austria—constitute today a unique type of hybrid

transitional society in the process of transformation, with features that are as yet so fluid and lacking precision that it is extremely difficult to summarize its fundamental nature in a concise formula.

The most exact definition that can be given of the social nature of these countries is a definition *by description*. These countries appear to have a society in which:

a. The transition between capitalism and Soviet society has resulted not from a proletarian revolution, but from a military-political overturn which eliminated the big bourgeoisie and the bulk of the middle bourgeoisie;

b. Capitalist survival subsists only in small industry and in commerce;

c. Agriculture remains capitalist in property relations (no nationalization of land) as well as in the dominant mode of exploitation (small private property);

d. Foreign trade, a state monopoly in fact if not in law, cannot free itself from the pressure and the attractive force of the world capitalist market, as a consequence of an insufficient material base for even bureaucratic planning, in each one of these countries;

e. Beside the peasantry, a germinator of capitalist forces, there is a proletariat which has had no important part in the crystallization of the new social situation and which for this reason has no important subjective ties with the present state, except in Yugoslavia;

f. The formation of a native bureaucratic layer around the PC bureaucracy in power, with some rare exceptions, is only in the initial stage;

g. The Bonapartist and extreme police form of the state reflects both its historic origins and the present prostration of the fundamental classes in society;

h. Nevertheless, this Bonapartist form of the state differs from classical Bonapartism (in the last analysis, the instrument of the bourgeoisie) and at the same time from Soviet Bonapartism (the instrument of a workers' bureaucracy in a postcapitalist society), and constitutes above all else an instrument of domination by the Soviet bureaucracy, the expression of an *international* relationship of forces which is superimposed on the given class relationships and which distorts their normal expression.

7. What are the factors determining the social difference between the buffer countries and the USSR?

a. On the economic plane: The nationalization of big industry, the banks, the means of communication and of wholesale trade has created *necessary* but insufficient conditions for planning, even in a degenerated bureaucratic form as in the USSR. The narrow national framework within which each one of the buffer countries is enclosed; their lack of sufficient material resources to develop the productive forces; the mortgage the Soviet bureaucracy has imposed on the economy of these countries; the predominantly agricultural character of these countries which, without nationalization of the soil and under the predominant regime of small private exploitation, reproduce capitalism from day to day on a village scale; the dependence of these countries on the world capitalist market, for the material means of their industrialization—the sum of all these factors creates a situation in which the major part of the production of these countries is still destined for a *capitalist* market—whether it is internal or external. For this very reason it is subject to the influences of all the oscillations of the world capitalist conjuncture and to the process of equalization of the average rate of profit. The conditions of fusion between the petty-bourgeois peasant market, state industry and the world capitalist market, which Lenin and Trotsky designated as a danger for the USSR in the period of the NEP, is today the determining situation in the buffer countries. This is expressed by the fact that in the advanced buffer countries (Poland, Czechoslovakia, Hungary) foreign trade embraces approximately half of the national revenue and that not only today, but even in 1952 (according to the present plans), more than half of this trade will be with the Western countries, from which the decisive elements for the industrialization of these countries must come. This is likewise expressed by the fact that these countries were obliged in almost all cases to *reimburse* foreign capital for its property nationalized in the buffer countries and to *recognize* the old debts, thus imposing an additional weight on their economy already strained to the extreme.

b. On the *social* plane: The fact that the present situation did not come about as a result of a victorious proletarian revolution, but as a result of the military-political successes achieved by the Soviet bureaucracy against the bourgeoisie as well as against the proletariat; the fact also that the formation of a bureaucratic caste is as yet only in the initial stage—both lead to the conclusion that, with the exception of Yugoslavia, it is very unlikely, if not excluded, that a *civil war* would be necessary to reverse the present orientation of these countries towards a structural assimilation with the USSR. The same applies also to the *state structure.* With the exception of Yugoslavia, the state apparatus of the buffer zone did not result from violent destruction of the old bourgeois state apparatus, but from its "conquest" by the Stalinist parties, with the aid of Russian pressure and a series of successive purges. It follows that this apparatus is even today saturated with bourgeois and petty-bourgeois elements, especially in the army cadres, in diplomacy and in the management of the economy. In the period which followed the October Revolution, proletarian control over the bourgeois cadres in the service of the workers state, as well as the democracy in the Bolshevik party, acted as a brake on the detrimental influence of these elements on the conduct of the state and the economy. At the present stage in the buffer zone, which came about not as a result of a proletarian revolution but of bureaucratic maneuvers, such control is completely absent, strengthening thereby the weight of the bourgeois elements in the apparatus, which likewise reflects the structural differences between the economy of the buffer countries and that of the USSR. It may also be said that the return of the buffer countries into the capitalist orbit would not necessitate the destruction of the present state apparatus, but a "purge" in a reverse sense.

c. On the *political* plane: The fate of the buffer countries has not yet been decided, not alone in the historical sense as in the case of the USSR, but in a much more immediate sense. The totality of the present world political currents: The Marshall Plan, the relative "reconstruction" of Western Germany, American rearmament, the economic perspectives of American imperialism and of the Soviet Five-Year Plan, the development of the proletarian struggles and those of the colonial peoples—all these factors will decide in the coming months the *immediate* fate of the buffer countries. As indicated by the political and strategic plans of imperialism and of the Stalinist bureaucracy, it is very improbable if not excluded that it is necessary to have a *war* in order to lead back some of these countries of the buffer zone into the imperialist orbit. This reason, added to those indicated above, makes it appear erroneous to modify as of today our evaluation of the social nature of these countries, except to indicate clearly the processes of their structural assimilation with the USSR and the stages already realized in this assimilation. This is why the tasks of the Fourth International in these countries remain, in a general way, those enumerated by the Second World Congress. Only in the eventuality described in Point 9 would a revision become necessary.

8. This whole description leads to the conclusion that the buffer zone, except for Finland and the Russian-occupied zones in Austria and Germany, are *on the road* toward structural assimilation with the USSR, but that this assimilation has not yet been accomplished. The social differences between the USSR and the buffer zone, enumerated above, are of a *qualitative* nature even though from the *quantitative* point of view society in the buffer zone approaches more closely Soviet society rather than that of the "normal" capitalist countries, in the same sense in which the USSR itself is quantitatively closer to capitalism than to socialism. Only in this sense can we continue to define the buffer countries as *capitalist countries on the road toward structural assimilation with the USSR.* This definition, necessarily awkward and too concise to embrace the different aspects of the buffer zone, thus signifies essentially that in the course of the process of the structural assimilation of these countries the dialectical leap has not yet been produced. It stresses both the historic origins of the present situation, as well as the social physiognomy which is as yet undecided. But it does not at all imply that the bourgeoisie is in power as the dominant class in these countries. This definition implies that the situation in the buffer countries likewise differs from the situation in a "normal" and "classic" capitalist society. It serves exclusively to denote the place of these countries in relation both to capitalism and the USSR, since Marxist sociology excludes the existence of economies and states that are neither capitalist nor Soviet (workers

or degenerated workers).

9. To what extent can this structural assimilation be completed, so that it will be necessary to modify our appreciation of the social nature of the buffer zone? The factors enumerated above indicate at the same time the concrete obstacles to the completion of this assimilation and the conditions under which this assimilation would be effectively completed. All these can be reduced to one factor: The achievement of effective coordination and planning applied to the combined economies of these countries linked organically to the economy of the USSR. Such an achievement could reverse the present predominant tendency of these countries to depend upon capitalist economy. This could happen, for instance, in the case of the abolition of national frontiers between the various buffer countries.

The existence of these frontiers, in effect, greatly limits the material base on which planned economy can be constructed and requires, at the same time, the maintenance of a series of state apparatuses which, as a result of their origins, cannot but be saturated with bourgeois elements. At the same time, the abolition of national frontiers would give a real impulsion to the development of the productive forces and would constitute a progressive act of great historical importance, even if it was brought about by the conservative Stalinist bureaucracy. It would really be comparable, in Trotsky's words, to the unification of Germany by Bismarck and the House of Hohenzollern. Such an abolition of the frontiers, whether it is accomplished by the incorporation of some or all these countries in the USSR, or by the constitution of a Balkan-Danube Federation formally independent from the USSR, provided it forms a genuine unified framework for economic planning, could be defined as the decisive point, in the process of structural assimilation of these countries with the USSR, at which the social nature of these countries becomes qualitatively transformed.

On the plane of the state that would require the disappearance of the present hybrid state apparatus and the constitution of a state apparatus of a new type, copied no doubt from that of the USSR. In relation to this achievement, other modifications in the situation will have to be evaluated in the same sense: Eventual nationalization of the soil, incipient collectivization of the land, establishment of a plan for the joint economic development of all the buffer countries, reversal of the economic and commercial relations with the West, etc.

All the preceding constitutes a probable variant of an *objective historical process* and not at all a desirable goal for action by the revolutionary proletariat. In setting forth the conditions under which assimilation of the buffer zone to Russian society could be achieved by *Stalinist action,* the Fourth International—while modifying its attitude towards the buffer zone in case of war, should such a change come about—does not in the least relent in its struggle against the police oppression of the buffer zone masses by the Soviet bureaucracy and its agents. Precisely under the conditions of the development indicated above, the struggle of the Fourth International for independent Polish, Czech, Hungarian, etc., Soviet Republics will take on its full significance linked to a merciless denunciation of all the elements of national oppression that the bureaucracy introduces and will introduce in the buffer zone. As against the Stalinist perspective of the bureaucratic integration of the buffer zone within the USSR, the Fourth International develops before the buffer zone masses the revolutionary perspective of the integration of independent socialist Soviet republics within an independent Balkan-Danube Federation and within the Socialist United States of Europe.

### III. The special cases

10. In the case of those countries which are part of the USSR's "strategic buffer" but have at the same time undergone a separate economic and political evolution, the contradictory, combined, uneven character of the entire buffer zone development is most striking. The case of these countries indicates likewise how necessary it is to guard against hasty generalizations, how important it is to follow step by step the actual evolution of the situation in each particular country. In the case of *Yugoslavia* we have one extremity of the spectrum composed of all the nuances differentiating the situation in each one of the buffer countries. Yugoslavia, of all the buffer countries, was the only one in which the liquidation of the bulk of the possessing classes, as well as the destruction of the bourgeois state apparatus, took place by means of *mass*

*action,* that is, the guerrilla warfare which in this country took on the character of a genuine civil war. From this fundamental difference between Yugoslavia and the other buffer countries flow specific differences on a number of planes: The CP has a real base among the masses; the masses have a fundamentally different attitude to the new state; the Yugoslav CP has different relations toward the Soviet bureaucracy; there is the possibility of a real differentiation in the workers' movement following the Tito crisis, despite the undeniable existence of a police regime in this country. Even though the sum of these factors does not eliminate any of the structural obstacles to real planning and for this reason leaves Yugoslav economy as yet qualitatively different from the Russian economy, it undoubtedly brings this country closer, on the social and political plane, to the Soviet structure. The defense of Yugoslavia against the campaign of calumny, the economic blockade, etc., on the part of the Soviet bureaucracy must be considered within the framework of our evaluation of the workers' movement of this country, the origins of its state, and the revolutionary possibilities opened up as a consequence of this workers' movement and the origins of this state, which take precedence over purely economic considerations.

11. *Finland* lies at the other end of the spectrum of the buffer zone. There we have a bourgeoisie which has hardly been shaken by the war and which formally retains control of its economic and state positions. There we have a proletariat which is much more developed and, as a consequence of a number of historical developments, less susceptible to Stalinist maneuvers. There also we find more resolute imperialist support for the Finnish bourgeoisie than for any other bourgeoisie in the buffer zone. Consequently, the Stalinist bureaucracy limits itself in Finland to the imposition of economic tribute and to the occupation of certain strategic positions, leaving the rest of the country to evolve within the framework of a quasi-normal bourgeois economy. This has had its political reflection in a consolidation of the conservative forces, culminating after the inevitable transition period in the expulsion of the Stalinists from the coalition government and in the elimination of the erstwhile positions they had conquered in the state apparatus following the military victory of the USSR. The evolution of Finland cannot, of course, be considered any more definitive than that of the rest of the buffer zone. The international situation can compel the bureaucracy to increase its pressure on this country and can lead to a new desperate effort at military resistance. The Finnish case is important, however, above all because it shows that the bureaucracy did not attempt to impose, or succeed in imposing, on all of the buffer zone a unified scheme of development and because it illustrates the fact that a certain *internal* conjuncture, a certain prostration of the fundamental social classes, was one of the necessary conditions for even the temporary success of the Stalinist maneuvers in the buffer zone.

12. The *Austrian* zone of occupation approximates Finland very closely. The Soviet bureaucracy was obliged to limit itself to the seizure of several economic stakes (former German property) and the occupation of important strategic positions. But it was in no position to influence the general economic orientation of Austria which evolved within the framework of a normal capitalist economy included within the Marshall Plan. Nor could it influence the social and political developments, which led to elimination from power, and culminated in a normalization and a strengthening of bourgeois power. As in the Finnish case, the international relationship of forces was the decisive factor in this evolution. But the concrete relationship between the classes was likewise the major obstacle to the Stalinist maneuvers.

Finally, the *German* zone of occupation constitutes another special case, situated midway between that of the buffer zone in general and that of Austria. The decisive characteristic of the situation in Eastern Germany lies in the fact that the most important industrial sector has been seized by the USSR and has been transformed into Soviet property. Parallel with this, there has been large scale dismantlement. Nationalizations have affected, aside from the Russian sector of the economy, an important part but not all of big industry and wholesale trade. There has remained a middle bourgeoisie, which drains a considerable part of the national income. Finally, the formation of a bureaucratic layer rising over the proletariat, and acting as the extended arm of the Russian bureaucracy, is in that country much more advanced than in the other buffer countries. If the situation in Eastern Germany remains indecisive, it is because more than any other country of the buffer zone, it depends in the first place on the international situation. That is, on the eventual solution of the German problem in its entirety and the specific orientation of the USA and the USSR in relation to this problem. It still cannot be said whether the Soviet bureaucracy has decided to retain its positions in Eastern Germany at all costs or whether it will be ready to consider them as bargaining points in order to retain the rest of the buffer zone and in order to obtain a certain influence on the entirety of German affairs (the slogan of unification, etc.). Under these conditions, the status of this zone of occupation as well as the direction of its development remain more fluid than is the case in the rest of the buffer zone, and the tendency to structural assimilation with the USSR is less pronounced there.

From the point of view of our tasks, the Fourth International continues to defend there the theses of the World Congress and considers that all measures of the Soviet bureaucracy, including eventual incorporation of Eastern Germany within a Balkan-Danube Federation—which is very doubtful—must be combatted and regarded as reactionary in relation to the destruction of German unity and the paralysis of the German proletariat that would result therefrom.

## IV. The theoretical significance of the buffer zone development

13. The appearance of *new transitional regimes,* as is the case of the buffer countries, regimes of transition between capitalism and the USSR, is not the result of chance nor the effect of negligible historical accidents. Only incurable pedants can conceive of capitalism and socialism as fixed entities, established once and for all, to which a living historic process must conform, a process contradictory and rich in the crystallization of ever new combined forms. In reality, the appearance of mixed transitional regimes and their combined character is the clearest expression of our historic epoch, which is defined by:

a. An ever more advanced disintegration of capitalism;

b. The conditions of extended delay of the world revolution, essentially the result of the counterrevolutionary Stalinist leadership of the world labor movement;

c. The existence of the USSR not only as a power continuing to polarize the revolutionary aspirations of an important part of the world proletariat, but also as a state power having a military-political weight of its own and with a logic of expansion of its own.

Only in the light of these three factors can the appearance and the development of a new and combined phenomenon like that of the Soviet buffer zone be understood and the limits of its real historic import be defined.

14. Ascertaining the existence of such transitional regimes does not at all upset our evaluation of the counterrevolutionary role of Stalinism nor our evaluation of Stalinism as a disintegrating force in the USSR and as a force organizing defeats of the world proletariat:

a. An evaluation of Stalinism cannot be made on the basis of localized results of its policy but must proceed from the entirety of its action on a world scale. When we consider the state of decay which capitalism presents even today, four years after the end of the war, and when we consider the concrete situation of 1943–1945, there can be no doubt that Stalinism, on a world scale, appeared as the decisive factor in preventing a sudden and simultaneous crash of the capitalist order in Europe and in Asia. In this sense, the "successes" achieved by the bureaucracy in the buffer zone constitute, at most, the price which imperialism paid for services rendered on the world arena—a price which is moreover constantly called into question at the following stage.

b. From the world point of view, the reforms realized by the Soviet bureaucracy in the sense of an assimilation of the buffer zone to the USSR weigh incomparably less in the balance than the blows dealt by the Soviet bureaucracy, especially through its actions in the buffer zone, against the consciousness of the world *proletariat,* which it demoralizes, disorients and paralyzes by all of its politics and thus renders it susceptible to some extent to the imperialist campaign of war preparations. Even from the point of view of the USSR itself, the defeats and the demoralization of the world proletariat caused by Stalinism constitute an incomparably greater danger than the consolidation of the buffer zone constitutes a reenforcement.

c. In the buffer zone itself, where objective as well as subjective conditions were ripe for an immediate overthrow of capitalism in 1943–1944, Stalinist policy has led to the temporary strengthening of the antiproletarian forces, created a thousand new obstacles on the way to the abolition of capitalism and thus caused the whole painful and jerky process of assimilation, dragging this process out over a number of years and rendering the proletariat in the main apathetic and even hostile, whereas the revolutionary movement of the proletariat could have achieved the liquidation of capitalism in these countries in a much shorter time and with a minimum of overhead charges.

d. As a result of the very expansion of the Soviet bureaucracy under the concrete conditions noted above, the objective contradictions in the situation of the buffer zone tend to penetrate into the very heart of the bureaucracy and of Soviet economy, multiplying the tensions and antagonisms which already exist within them abundantly, and to prepare the ground for the development of manifold centrifugal tendencies (Tito tendency on the one hand, Gomulka-Akerman tendency on the other).

15. Historically, the above-mentioned conditions not only indicate the reasons for the appearance of transitional regimes but also circumscribe the limits of the viability of the Soviet bureaucracy:

a. On the *social* plane, the overthrow of the Soviet bureaucracy remains certain within the framework of a world decision in the class struggle, which is inevitable one way or another in the long run.

b. On the *military-political* plane, this overthrow remains equally inevitable if the world proletariat does not succeed in crushing imperialism in time, with such an eventuality also entailing the downfall of the bureaucracy.

The appearance of transitional regimes of the buffer zone type thus merely gives expression to the *interlude* character of the historic period proceeding from 1943 up to the present: an interlude between the low point of the worldwide decline of the proletarian revolution and the new world revolutionary upsurge, which has only been seen in its rough outlines up to the present; an interlude between the Second World War and the final clash between imperialism and the USSR. Only within the framework of this limited interlude do the buffer zone and all the phenomena associated with it appear in their true light as provisional and temporary. And in this framework, the real nature of Stalinism appears more pronounced than ever in the sense indicated by the Fourth International.

# REMARKS BY M. STEIN OPENING POLITICAL COMMITTEE DISCUSSION ON INTERNATIONAL EXECUTIVE COMMITTEE RESOLUTION ON EASTERN EUROPE

## *Political Committee meeting, July 12, 1949*

The extension of the power of the Soviet bureaucracy beyond the borders of the USSR, which was one of the consequences of World War II, has posed the following questions: (1) Does the basic Trotskyist analysis of the Kremlin bureaucracy retain its validity under the new conditions of Stalinist expansion? and (2) What is the nature of the regimes established by the bureaucracy in the new territory it acquired?

These questions were the subject of an extensive discussion in the world Trotskyist movement which came to a close at the World Congress in April 1948 with the adoption of the thesis on "The USSR and Stalinism." However, the Seventh Plenum of the IEC, which in its representation and deliberations almost had the weight of a world congress decided to reopen a discussion in the International on the nature of the buffer countries.

This was motivated by two considerations: (1) The year 1948 witnessed a new phase in Stalinist policy in these countries, which requires an analysis and the education of the ranks in an understanding of this problem. (2) Some shadings of difference developed among the supporters of the World Congress Thesis which required an airing. Namely, while there was general agreement at the Seventh Plenum on the totality of the buffer countries, some comrades felt that Yugoslavia belongs in a category by itself for reasons I shall deal with later. I am not dealing with the position of the British RCP which represents no new factor in the discussion, since its point of view was already presented to the World Congress and overwhelmingly rejected by it.

In introducing the discussion it is best to start with a summary of the evaluation of the buffer zone as contained in both the World Congress Thesis and the Seventh Plenum resolutions. The plenum resolution is only an extension of the World Congress document. It brings the situation up to date within the framework of the basic analysis made at the World Congress.

The fortunes of war left the Stalinist bureaucracy as the undisputed heir to the Balkan countries excepting Greece, parts of Austria, Finland and Eastern Germany, Manchuria, and Northern Korea in Asia. They inherited these countries in which the state apparatus had collapsed as a result of the war, military defeats, Nazi occupation, the guerrilla war, Russian occupation, etc. The possessing classes in these countries had been extremely weakened or had virtually disappeared.

Anglo-American imperialism was in no position to intervene and had abandoned the impotent bourgeoisie of these countries to the mercy of the Stalinist bureaucracy. From 1944 to 1946 this non-intervention corresponded to the agreements arrived at at Teheran, Yalta and Potsdam and constituted the price world imperialism paid Stalin for crushing the German proletariat and for his active aid in strangling the insurgent Greek and Italian movements and for reconstructing the capitalist states and economies of the Western European countries.

Following 1946 the imperialist powers failed to come to the aid of the bourgeoisies in the buffer countries, because the relationship of forces, both military and political on the European continent, were as yet unfavorable for a showdown fight. They had to confine themselves to the so-called Cold War.

What did the Stalinist bureaucracy do with the countries and their peoples—with their political

From SWP *Internal Bulletin*, Vol. XI, No. 5, October 1949, pages 14–18.

and economic structure—over which it was now the master? A review of the Stalinist course will bring into bold relief the contradictory nature of the counterrevolutionary nationally-limited bureaucratic caste resting on the foundation of nationalized property relations created by the October Revolution.

The first stage of Stalinist policy is characterized by the crushing of all initiative by the masses. Towards this end it deliberately promoted national hatred and chauvinism between the countries within its own orbit and between all of them, on the one hand, against the Germans on the other. The Stalinists retraced the national boundaries and uprooted over ten million people in the process expelling them from one country into the other. The Germans were expelled from Eastern Prussia, Upper Silesia and the Sudeten area. Rumanians were expelled from Bessarabia, Poles were expelled by the Russians from the area east of the Curzon line, Czechs were expelled from Carpathia, Hungarians were expelled by the Czechs from South Slavia, etc.

They concluded alliances with the most reactionary forces in the buffer countries—Rumanian Court, Finnish bourgeoisie, semifascist Bulgarian formations, national democrats in Poland, etc. Any manifestation of working-class opposition was repressed. Whatever remnants of the bourgeoisie could be found were drawn into a national front to constitute the framework of capitalist states.

The economic policy of the Stalinist bureaucracy in the buffer countries consisted of merciless pillage of their resources through reparations, mixed corporations, seizure of so-called German property and phony trade agreements. In addition, these countries had to pay the cost of maintaining the Soviet occupation troops and in the case of Germany of forced labor by prisoners of war. The policy of pillage was practiced not only against the countries which had been at war with Russia, such as Hungary and Rumania, but also against "allied" countries, such as Czechoslovakia where some 60 large plants were dismantled. From the German territory ceded to Poland Stalin removed some 25–30 percent of all industrial tools, according to Minc, the Polish Minister of Industrial Production. Each one of the buffer countries was left more or less in this period to its own depleted resources as far as economic reconstruction was concerned.

Nationalizations at this stage were limited to enterprises seized by the workers at the end of the war, where there were no legal owners in the country. Otherwise the bourgeoisie retained its economic position. The Stalinist bureaucracy and the Stalinist parties sought to utilize capitalist production relations for their own advantage.

It was only after the Marshall Plan took form and the Kremlin was compelled to ban the participation of its satellite countries in the plan, that the Soviet bureaucracy turned its attention toward the consolidation of its dominant positions in Eastern Europe on a long-range basis. It was forced thus to counteract U.S. efforts to push the Russian bureaucracy back into the confines of the USSR.

The exigencies of the Cold War forced the Kremlin bureaucracy to undertake the liquidation of the strong positions of the native bourgeoisie in the buffer countries—to make an effort to develop these countries economically, to seek to limit Kulak grip on agriculture, and to undertake some sort of planning.

Great changes have taken place in the buffer countries within the past year. Industry, banking, communication, transportation have been almost completely nationalized in Bulgaria, Yugoslavia and Czechoslovakia—they are on the road to completion in Poland and Hungary. Wholesale trade is equally on the road to complete statification. Retail trade and agriculture remain, however, as yet largely in the hands of private proprietors. The private exploitation of agriculture is extremely important for Eastern Europe affecting a large segment of the population: about 80% of the people in Bulgaria and Rumania, about 70% in Yugoslavia, about 50% in Hungary, Poland and Czechoslovakia.

Any attempt at planning in the buffer countries has the obstacle of capitalist relations in agriculture, the Soviet mortgage on the economies of these countries in the form of reparations, mixed companies, etc., the narrow national limits of each of the countries, the apathy and even the passive hostility of the proletariat. The Stalinist bureaucracy which started out in the buffer countries with a policy of pillage and exploitation on the basis of capitalist property relations has been compelled in time to change its course and to seek to bring the economies of these countries into conformity with that of the USSR.

At every stage of development it had to resort to new police measures against recalcitrants. Not only did it destroy all opposition parties but it had to carry out successive purges of its own agents when they gave the slightest expressions to the sentiment of resistance to Stalinist policy. The whole course of the Stalinist bureaucracy in the buffer countries shows once more that it has no historical perspective, that it cannot pursue a fundamental orientation, but reacts empirically to the situation of the moment.

The resolution summarizes this policy as follows:

"Because it wanted first of all to strangle all possibility of a proletarian revolution it was led to conclude a temporary compromise with the bourgeoisie; because its privileges are historically incompatible with the maintenance of the capitalist regime, it had to take the course of the gradual and bureaucratic liquidation of the capitalist forces in the buffer zone."

There are indications that a new stage in Stalinist policy is in the making. There are signs of growing economic coordination between the different countries and the constitution of the Council of Mutual Aid, etc. These come in response to the Tito split and the Marshall Plan.

The plenum resolution on the social nature of the buffer countries comes to the conclusion that they are *capitalist countries on the road toward structural assimilation with the USSR.* This definition takes into account the historical origin of the situation as well as the social physiognomy which is as yet undecided. It tries to fix the position of these countries between capitalism and the USSR.

### Differences between buffer countries and the USSR

1. Necessary but insufficient conditions for planning, even in degenerated bureaucratic form: (a) narrow national framework; (b) lack of material resources; (c) mortgage imposed by Soviet bureaucracy; (d) predominantly agricultural character, which remains under small private exploitation and reproduces capitalism from day to day on the village scale.

2. The dependence of these countries on the world capitalist market—Poland, Czechoslovakia and Hungary—foreign trade embraces about half the national revenue—and even by 1952 according to present plans—more than half of this trade will be with Western countries.

3. The fact that changes did not come about as a result of victorious revolutions but by military-political measures against the bourgeoisie and the proletariat leads to the conclusion that—with the exception of Yugoslavia—it is unlikely that a civil war would be necessary to reverse the present orientation in these countries. The return of these countries to the capitalist orbit would not require the destruction of the present state apparatus, but a "purge" in reverse.

The fate of the buffer countries has not been decided not only in historical sense, as in the case of the USSR, but in a more immediate sense. The resolution indicates under what conditions it would be necessary to modify the above definition and say that structural assimilation has been completed. This would require above all that there be effective coordination and planning applied to the combined economies of these countries linked organically to the economy of the USSR. Such an achievement could reverse the present predominant tendency of these countries of dependence upon capitalist economy. This could happen if the national frontiers were abolished. It would require the disappearance of the hybrid state apparatuses—saturated with bourgeois elements—and the constitution of a state apparatus of a new type.

As I indicated, the differences expressed at the plenum were of a two-fold character:

1. There were some—namely Jerome, Silva, and Ali—who, while accepting the fundamental line of the resolution, thought that Yugoslavia should be treated in a different category. Jerome's argument essentially boils down to this:

a. The state apparatus there was destroyed by the independent action of the masses.

b. The bourgeoisie was largely expropriated in the process of a protracted civil war.

c. When the resolution says, "It is very unlikely if not excluded that a *civil war* would be necessary to reverse the present orientation of these countries towards a structural assimilation with the USSR" it specifically excludes Yugoslavia.

While making all these distinctions between Yugoslavia and the other buffer countries the resolution nevertheless fails to draw conclusions. In Jerome's opinion it was necessary to conclude that in Yugoslavia—unlike the other buffer countries—capitalism has been destroyed.

2. De Silva argued that it has been precisely the policy of the Kremlin bureaucracy, whose economic and political measures are designed to exploit the buffer countries, which has blocked the tendency of these countries towards structural assimilation with the Soviet Union. But Yugoslavia, by breaking with the Soviet bureaucracy, has liberated itself from these fetters and can be considered a workers state.

It appears to me that while there is much truth in both these arguments they cannot, nevertheless, be isolated from the totality of the picture. The unstable equilibrium in the relations between the Soviet bureaucracy and capitalist world places Yugoslavia in a particularly vulnerable position. In the meantime it remains a fact that in Yugoslavia as well agriculture, which embraces 70 percent of the people, remains capitalist in character.

Rather than jumping at conclusions as to the social character of the states in Eastern Europe it is far better to await further development. This is especially important when dealing with such hybrid formations directed by bureaucracies whose main concern is with survival and who are capable of all sorts of sharp turns in their struggle to retain police power *at all costs.*

# THE PROBLEM OF EASTERN EUROPE

By Joseph Hansen

It has been felt by some comrades that the differences over the characterization of the class structure of such countries in Eastern Europe as Yugoslavia may turn out to be purely terminological and that we who want to call them "workers states," at bottom assess the developments in the same way as those who insist on calling them "capitalist countries on the road toward structural assimilation with the USSR."

This may be the case. The differences may concern only what is the most appropriate label to place on the highly complex and rapidly changing reality we see in Eastern Europe.

However, it would be a great mistake to assume that the differences are merely terminological. We are dealing here with the touchstone of the proletarian revolution and the heart of Marxist politics—the class character of the state. When we deal with this question, the utmost scientific scrupulousness is required of us.

In the history of our movement, we have seen currents alien to Marxism arise again and again over differences involving this question. While such differences do not always indicate the development of an anti-Marxist trend, experience demands that we check our conclusions with the greatest strictness and seek to discover why the differences have arisen.

The discussion thus should be educational. We are under no pressure to bring it to a hasty conclusion. We have time to think things through to the end.

The developments in Eastern Europe are of the utmost importance to the future of our movement. They test our capacity to apply Marxist theory to the most contradictory and dynamic phenomena. They offer the most encouraging political perspectives for the growth of our movement, for the possibility of constructing a lever and a fulcrum for toppling the counterrevolutionary Stalinist bureaucracy that constitutes the main obstacle in the world labor movement to socialist revolution. Belgrade's break with Moscow is only the first major indication of the profound opposition to the Kremlin welling up throughout this whole area.

We can now see how the fruits of Soviet victories over world imperialism tend not only to temporarily strengthen the Stalinist bureaucracy but also to undermine its position. We can understand more fully why Trotsky was so concerned about our following developments in the ranks of Stalinism in full expectation of deep splits and the appearance of currents that can move in our direction.

A correct analysis of the class character of the Eastern European countries should help us win this new opposition movement to the banner of Trotskyism and thereby hasten the debacle of Stalinism.

### The theses of the Second World Congress

First of all, let us consider some of the propositions in the theses adopted by the Second World Congress of the Fourth International in April of last year.

"It is not excluded," one of the theses states, "that a certain relation of forces may necessitate a real structural assimilation of one or another country in the 'buffer zone.' But it is necessary to indicate clearly that the policy of the step-by-step limitation of the privately-owned sectors of industry has not been oriented in this direction up to now. And the specific forms of exploitation introduced by the Soviet bureaucracy constitute entirely new and powerful obstacles to structural assimilation." (*Fourth International*, June 1948, pp. 118–119.)

From this April 1948 thesis we can draw the conclusion that while this or that country might be assimilated into the USSR, the trend was definitely not in that direction. The limitation of privately-owned sectors was not "oriented" that way and the Stalinist bureaucracy was introducing "new and powerful obstacles" to it.

The thesis declares, however: "This situation can only be *transitional.* It must end either in the bureaucracy's withdrawal from its position, under the pressure of imperialism, or in the real destruction of capitalism, which can take place only as a result of the revolutionary mobilization of the masses, and the elimination of the special forms of exploitation, introduced by the bureaucracy in their countries."

This seems quite clear. Either the Kremlin must withdraw from the countries of Eastern Europe or it must undertake a "real destruction of capitalism." This real destruction of capitalism "can take place only as a result of the revolutionary mobilization of the masses."

I for one took the "real destruction of capitalism" to mean an overturn in property relations, the ending of private property relations, the ending of private property in the means of production and the institution of state-owned property. This would lay the foundation of a workers state in these countries and, with the establishment of common property forms, would open up the road to assimilation within the framework of the degenerated workers state.

The means for achieving this overturn in property relations was categorically specified as the "revolutionary mobilization of the masses" and from the way it is put in the theses it would seem clear that this revolutionary mobilization had not yet occurred as of April 1948. In fact the Stalinist bureaucracy had done everything to stamp out such spontaneous mobilizations as had broken out.

The theses, however, did place a question mark over the necessity of a revolutionary mobilization, declaring that "a destruction of this sort did take place in the Baltic countries, Eastern Poland, Bessarabia, Karelia . . ." It is not made clear precisely what happened in these countries. We are told only that "this was possible owing to the relationship of forces inside the labor movement and the degree of control exercised by the Stalinists over the mass movement. The bourgeoisie here was, moreover, extremely enfeebled and found itself caught between the pressure of world imperialism, on the one hand, and of the bureaucracy on the other."

One could wonder if the theses do not concede in principle that a revolutionary mobilization of the masses is *not* required, given the conditions that the Stalinists control the mass movement, the bourgeoisie is enfeebled and world imperialism cannot come to its aid.

In any case, the theses emphasized that for the other Eastern European countries the destruction of capitalism "is impossible without a revolutionary mobilization of the masses."

The slogans elaborated for use in these countries were aimed at mobilizing the masses against the Stalinists and against the capitalist state. Among the demands were "Expropriation of the big and middle bourgeoisie," "Expropriation of foreign capital," "Real planning through the centralization of the industries and banks in trusts and in a state Bank," "Elaboration of a plan for harmonious economic development between city and country, in the interest of the masses, with the active participation of workers and poor peasants committees."

The theses declared that, "The fact that capitalism still exists in these countries side by side with exploitation by the Stalinist bureaucracy must fundamentally determine our strategy. The capitalist nature of these countries imposes the necessity of the strictest revolutionary defeatism in war time."

It was emphasized that against the Stalinists and against the native bourgeois elements we are for the independent strategy that finds its essential support in the world forces of the socialist revolution. "The fundamental aim of our strategy thus remains the establishment of Independent Socialist Republics of Poland, Czechoslovakia, Hungary, etc., within the framework of the Socialist United States of Europe."

Since the Socialist United States of Europe cannot be created at one stroke, it would seem that our immediate tactic in carrying out this strategy would be to fight for the establishment of Independent Socialist Republics which would try to extend their revolution as rapidly as possible.

It is interesting to note in passing that although the theses point out that the Stalinist bureaucracy has not nationalized the land and that "agriculture, which is preponderant in the economy of most of these countries, retains its capitalist structure," no slogan was listed calling for the nationalization of the land. This seems strange in view of the great stress which has since been laid upon this factor in determining the character of the economy as a whole.

Was it simply an oversight? Or did the comrades who drew up the theses feel at the time that this was not as crucial an issue as the others on which they did work out slogans?

It should also be observed that in calling for "real planning" the resolution could well be interpreted to mean planning within the capacities of an independent socialist republic.

### The resolution of the Seventh Plenum

Now let us turn to the resolution adopted for discussion one year later by the Seventh Plenum of the International Executive Committee of the Fourth International.

"Important changes have taken place in Eastern Europe during the year 1948," we are told. "The nationalization of industry, of the banking system, of communications and transport, have been practically completed in Bulgaria, in Yugoslavia and in Czechoslovakia; it is on the road to completion in Poland and in Hungary, and it has had a big start in Rumania. Wholesale trade is equally on the road to statification in most of these countries. Only retail trade and agriculture remain as yet largely in the hands of private proprietors."

Specifying what has happened in the various countries, the resolution declares that in Yugoslavia "the liquidation of the bulk of the possessing classes as well as the destruction of the bourgeois state apparatus took place by means of *mass action*, that is, the guerrilla warfare which in this country took on the character of a genuine civil war."

We cannot help agreeing that "important changes have taken place in Eastern Europe." One of the comrades who holds that the countries where such events have occurred still come under such a finished social category as "capitalism" has said that this resolution is "only an extension" of the document adopted by the World Congress last year. It may be an extension in the sense that it still designates countries where such changes have occurred as "capitalist" but most certainly the reality in Eastern Europe is no simple extension of what we had before. It seems obvious to me that a qualitative change in property relations has occurred which should be reflected in the resolution.

A number of most important questions are at once raised by these events. Is the breaking of the grip of the bourgeoisie in these countries progressive? Are the nationalizations in Eastern Europe a necessary step on the road to socialism? Does the capacity of Stalinism to engineer such major changes indicate our analysis of the Kremlin bureaucracy to be wrong? These questions have to be answered no matter what label you put on these countries as a result of the overturn in property relations.

But even more is in store. Outside of Yugoslavia where it is admitted a "genuine" civil war occurred, where was the revolutionary mobilization of the masses without which, according to the theses of only 12 months before, the destruction of capitalism is "impossible"?

The resolution states that the "resistance of the dying propertied classes in these countries" is up to now being "liquidated step by step by the Stalinists through 'cold' means, without any mobilization of the masses being required." The quotation marks around the "cold" are intended to indicate, I take it, that the process did not occur in deep freeze and may at times have been somewhat warm.

The explanation for these extraordinary happenings is the same as that offered the year before in the case of the Baltic countries, East Poland and Karelia. The imperialists did not intervene. They "practically abandoned their extremely weakened bourgeoisie to the crushing political and military superiority of the Stalinist bureaucracy."

Doesn't this raise in principle the question of whether or not the bourgeoisie can be expropriated, broken as a class, property relations overturned and economy nationalized without a revolutionary mobilization of the masses? It seems to me that this question *is* raised and that hastily placing such a finished social category as "capitalism" on the resulting economy doesn't help matters. You still have to answer these questions. Moreover, by calling it "capitalist" you raise additional complications.

Can such changes occur in other capitalist states? Does capitalism still have room for such progressive developments? Doesn't the alleged capacity of capitalism to make room for changes like these indicate that our analysis of the capitalist system contains a fundamental flaw?

This is not all that is called in question. If these satellite countries which are such evident replicas of the degenerated workers state are "capitalist" isn't the USSR "capitalist" or "state capitalist" as some comrades consider it? Where do you draw the line and precisely why? If it's only the revolutionary origin of the Soviet Union with what's left of the resulting reservoir of mass social and political consciousness that makes it a workers state and not the fundamental property relations, how much longer can that criterion be held to apply?

By attempting to stretch such a finished social category as "capitalism" to cover the qualitative change in property relations that has occurred in the countries listed in the resolution, it appears to me nothing is clarified. We only force ourselves to break away from the orthodox Marxist criteria in determining the character of a state. We force ourselves to introduce innovations in our theory that to me do not seem at all necessary or justified.

### Yugoslavia and 'real planning'

For instance, take the case of Yugoslavia. Here we have had a revolutionary mobilization of the masses; we have had a "genuine" civil war; the grip of the bourgeoisie has been broken, they are "disappearing"; the decisive sectors of the economy have been nationalized. Planning has been instituted. According to the November issue of *Fourth International* measures are being taken "to accelerate the preparations for the collectivization of agriculture." The regime is moving to the left.

Yet according to the new criterion laid down in the resolution of the Seventh Plenum, Yugoslavia cannot be characterized as a "workers state." "Why not?" we ask in astonishment. "Isn't there evidence enough that a qualitative change has occurred in property relations?"

Here's the answer given by the resolution: "The sum of these factors does not eliminate any of the structural obstacles to real planning and for this reason leaves Yugoslav economy as yet qualitatively different from the Russian economy."

The structural obstacles to "real planning" flow from the small area of Yugoslavia, its small population, its limited resources and its backwardness. These obstacles cannot be overcome until Yugoslavia can abolish its frontiers either by "incorporation" in the Soviet Union or in a "Balkan-Danube Federation formally independent from the USSR"—provided that the Balkan-Danube Federation "forms a genuine unified framework for economic planning."

If this occurs, then the incorporation "could be defined as the decisive point, in the process of structural assimilation of these countries with the USSR, at which the social nature of these countries becomes qualitatively transformed."

This constitutes *the* decisive criterion laid down by the resolution for determining whether or not Yugoslavia—and of course the other countries—can be considered workers states. Since this criterion has not been met we are therefore forced to conclude *ipso facto* that the buffer countries are "capitalist countries on the road toward structural assimilation with the USSR."

The resolution continues with the observation that, "This definition, necessarily awkward and too concise to embrace the different aspects of the buffer zone, thus signifies essentially that in the course of the process of the structural assimilation of these countries the dialectical leap has not yet been produced. It stresses both the historic origins of the present situation, as well as the social physiognomy which is as yet undecided. But it does not at all imply that the bourgeoisie is in power as the dominant class in these countries."

Note that last sentence: *"But it does not at all imply that the bourgeoisie is in power as the dominant class in these countries."* I take it that the comrades who drew up this resolution knew what they were doing. They are reporting their considered, joint conclusion as to the *fact* in the countries under analysis. But if the bourgeoisie is not in power as the dominant class "in these countries" what class then *is* in power?

By introducing the new criterion of "real planning," the resolution opens the door to the theory that we can have countries where the bourgeoisie has been smashed as the ruling class, a different class is in power, but which are still not workers states.

The resolution continues: "This definition implies that the situation in the buffer countries likewise differs from the situation in a 'normal' and 'classic' capitalist society. It serves exclusively to denote the place of these countries in relation both to capitalism and the USSR, since Marxist sociology excludes the existence of economies and states that are neither capitalist nor Soviet (workers or degenerated workers)."

I shall presently try to show that although Marxist sociology does exclude states and economies that are "neither" capitalist nor Soviet, it makes provision for states and economies that are *both* capitalist and Soviet. Right now I want to emphasize that we are dealing with an innovation so far as criteria is concerned, an innovation for which no justification is offered, the innovation of "real planning" as the decisive test in determining whether we have a workers state.

If we were to accept this innovation then we automatically exclude all small, backward, poverty-stricken countries from being designated as workers states so long as they remain isolated, no matter what overturns might be made in property relations. We could not, for example, call Bolivia a workers state if the workers and peasants smashed the grip of the feudalistic landlords and the mining oligarchy and set up their own government, for the simple reason that they could not possibly introduce "real planning." Bolivia by itself could never institute the "real planning" called for in the resolution. That would require the combined efforts of a number of South American countries at the very least.

Comrade Germain explains this point more fully in his article in the September *Fourth International*. He says that the Left Opposition drafted the first plan in the USSR against the violent resistance of the bureaucracy and of the Stalinist faction. "But it does not follow from this that *any* national framework whatever lends itself to planning on the mere condition that the proletariat had conquered power. It is obvious that a *minimum material base* is indispensable even to the preparatory work of socialist planning. To *make a start* in the building of socialism in Rumania, in Luxembourg or in Paraguay is an even more patent absurdity than to pretend that this construction is *being completed* in the USSR."

This point is essentially correct. For *socialist* planning you do need a minimum material base. But it seems to me that Comrade Germain should have added for the benefit of revolutionary-minded workers in Rumania, Luxembourg and Paraguay that they can still make a good start toward the goal of socialist planning by conquering power and setting up their own government. That would give them a workers state, and while this is a long way from *socialism,* still it is a most essential and decisive step in *making a start.*

Comrade Germain could not do this, however, without running up against the criterion laid down in the resolution that the qualitative point of change between a capitalist state and a workers state is the institution of "real planning" which is possible only on a minimum material basis which neither Rumania, Luxembourg nor Paraguay has available.

### What about the USSR?

This, however, raises a difficult question. Does even the Soviet Union have the minimum material basis for "real planning"? I don't think it does; and the resolution itself is forced to admit that Soviet planning "is itself the bureaucratic deformation of real socialist planning." The resolution does not amplify this point, but lets it go at that.

It seems to me we are forced to conclude that to take the criterion of "real planning" as the decisive test of a workers state, to make it nothing less than the *qualitative point of change in distinguishing such a state from a capitalist state* is not valid.

Why should it not be applied to the Soviet Union? If planning in the Soviet Union does not meet our subjective standard or what we consider to be the norm of "real planning" wouldn't we be obligated to bring into question our characterization of the Soviet Union as a degenerated workers state? And don't all of us have the right and the duty to ask why this criterion has been introduced at the present time and given such decisive weight? Shouldn't it be explained and justified?

It appears to me to be a dangerous criterion that can be particularly damaging politically to our movement in all the small countries. Isn't it better to retain the orthodox criteria? I feel that we should continue to explain as we have innumerable times that real socialist planning is possible only with the combined efforts of a number of countries, including at least one or two of the industrially advanced ones; but meanwhile we have the pressing task of establishing the workers states required as the minimum material basis for that planning.

### The crux of the discussion

The crux of the whole discussion thus is, in my opinion, what criteria do we use in distinguishing a workers state from a capitalist state? This is the nub of the dispute. If we can agree on that then we should have little difficulty in ironing out the differences.

If you can convince me that we should make "real planning" our decisive criterion, the point of qualitative change, the nodal point where all the quantitative changes pass over, then I would have no choice but to continue characterizing Yugoslavia as "capitalist" and if Yugoslavia is still "capitalist" it goes without saying that all the rest of the Eastern European countries remain "capitalist."

If we agree on a different criterion, however, as the decisive one, say the crushing of the bourgeoisie as a class and the nationalization of economy, then we would have to consider at least Yugoslavia as a "workers state" and determine the character of each of the others in accordance with the actual facts.

I think it has been fairly well established that the criterion of "real planning," advanced in the Plenum resolution as decisive in determining whether we have a workers state before us, does not hold up under examination.

Now we are faced with the problem of accounting for the origin of this criterion. I see one of two possibilities.

Those comrades who insist that all of Eastern Europe, including Yugoslavia, must be characterized as "capitalist" were hard put to find criteria that would apply to all these countries without any exceptions. This criterion looked good because obviously you don't have real planning and can't have any resemblance to it in these countries without assimilation into the USSR or the establishment of a Balkan-Danube Federation. Consequently, the introduction of this novel criterion enabled the comrades to solve the whole problem of the Eastern European countries at one sweeping stroke.

That's one possibility. The other is this:

The comrades did not distinguish sharply enough between our general category of "workers state" and our general category of "socialism." A careful reading of the official documents and of the writings in support of those documents, or constructed in accordance with their basic line on this question, will reveal, I believe, a kind of mingling of the two concepts, so that we get no clear distinction between them. Comrade Germain's discussion of the impossibility of making a start in building socialism in Rumania, Luxembourg or Paraguay is an instance.

If this conjecture at the source of the new criterion is correct, we also have a possible explanation for the extreme reluctance of many comrades to pin the label "workers state" on any of these countries. The label is too closely associated in their minds with categories properly belonging under the general heading of "socialism." They do not make a clear distinction between a workers state and a land of socialism. The penalty for that, however, is the inability to make a clear distinction between a workers state and capitalism.

However, whatever the source of the new criterion about "real planning" may be, it appears obvious to me that the comrades who have sponsored it will be forced to drop it as the discussion brings greater clarity into the questions facing us.

### The category of the 'workers state'

One of the easiest errors to slip into when considering this question is to make a kind of fetish of the category "workers state." All of us tend to think of it as something glorious that arose to put an end to the blood and filth of capitalism. To this day an aura surrounds the words "workers state" because of all associations with Lenin and Trotsky and the great emancipating struggle they led. We therefore find difficulty connecting it with anything base, and even when we insist on its degeneration in the USSR a brightness still clings to it. We want it to be something noble and great and inspiring.

This is one of the sources of the incapacity of many people to make a distinction between the workers state and the regime resting on it. The state which has won their adherence is seen in the image of Stalin.

Others who have learned to hate Stalin, turn

away from the workers state with as little true understanding. The attraction has simply turned into its opposite.

To make a scientific appraisal, however, we must learn to cut through the superficial appearance. The state should be regarded as expressing a relation between classes. It is a relation of coercion that takes the form mainly of a civil bureaucracy and armed forces. Through this apparatus one class coerces or oppresses another.

The expression of this relation is not limited to a fixed form. "The forms of bourgeois states are exceedingly variegated," Lenin said. He at once added, of course, that "their essence is the same: in one way or another, all these states are in the last analysis inevitably a *dictatorship of the bourgeoisie.*" Similarly, Lenin continues, "The transition from capitalism to communism will certainly bring a great variety and abundance of political forms, but the essence will inevitably be only one: *the dictatorship of the proletariat.*" (V.I. Lenin, "State and Revolution," in *Collected Works*, vol. 25, p. 413.)

The dictatorship of the bourgeoisie, as we all know, is based on private property in the means of production. To maintain this social relation it oppresses the working class.

The dictatorship of the proletariat begins with the elevation of the working class into a ruling class in place of the capitalists. The task of the new power is to end the social relation peculiar to the capitalist class. But this does not occur overnight. Even a model workers state is still nothing but a hangover of capitalist society. On top of this, a workers state is forced to maintain for a time, even in the best of circumstances, bourgeois modes of distributing the national income.

We have a contradictory reality—a state that is based on destruction of bourgeois property forms and the nationalization of economy but which still retains vestiges of capitalism.

When this state eventually begins to wither away as the productive forces expand and all danger of a capitalist restoration vanishes, then we can first begin to speak of socialism, the lower stage of communism. If we call a workers state "socialist" it is more because of its aims and tendencies than what it is when it first emerges from the womb of capitalism.

A workers state is a *transitional* state, transitional between capitalism and socialism.

A healthy workers state carries this transition through as rapidly as possible by extending the revolution along the international spiral. But history has forced us to include in our general category a workers state that is not healthy, one that is retrogressing toward capitalism. This degenerated workers state, spilling over the frontiers fixed at the close of World War I, has upset capitalist property relations in Eastern Europe and given rise to formations that are pretty much replicas of the USSR. Their fate is intimately bound up with that of the Soviet Union. If the USSR must be included in our general category of a workers state, I do not think it is incorrect to include Yugoslavia and the other Eastern European countries where the capitalists have been displaced as the ruling class.

### Social content and political form

In November 1937, Trotsky wrote a most illuminating article on the character of the USSR. The title is "Not a Workers and Not a Bourgeois State? Political Form and Social Content." This article was Trotsky's response to Burnham and Carter when they first brought out their doubts about the Soviet Union being a workers state.

Written in a pedagogical manner, it picks up the theoretical threads of the pamphlet written four years earlier, *The Soviet Union and the Fourth International*. Trotsky explains the difference between the economic and social content of a workers state and the variegated political forms that it can assume.*

Here is one of Trotsky's illuminating instances: "The domination of the Social Democracy in the State and in the Soviets (Germany 1918–1919) had nothing in common with the dictatorship of the proletariat inasmuch as it left bourgeois property inviolable. But the regime which guards the expropriated and nationalized property from imperialists is, independent of political forms, the dictatorship of the proletariat." You will note that Trotsky does not include "real planning" in his criteria. He says "the regime which guards the expropriated and nationalized property from imperialists." (This

* "Not a Workers' and Not a Bourgeois State?" can be found in *Writings of Leon Trotsky* [1937–38], pp. 74–88 [2018 printing]. The pamphlet "The Soviet Union and the Fourth International" was published under the title "The Class Nature of the Soviet State" in *Writings* [1933–34], pp. 133–62 [2020 printing].

and the quotations that follow on pages 35–36 can be found in *Writings [1937–38]*, pp. 76–88.)

By way of symmetry he shows why a fascist regime must be considered capitalist. "So long as fascism with its barbaric methods defends private property in the means of production, the state remains bourgeois under the fascist rule." I know that none of our comrades will disagree with this. I cite it only to show that Trotsky's decisive criterion for determining a capitalist state was the fact that its regime "defends private property in the means of production."

"Only the intrusion of a revolutionary or a counterrevolutionary force in property relations can change the class nature of the state," Trotsky emphasizes. Then he continues: "But does not history really know of cases of class conflict between the economy and the state? It does! When the Third Estate seized power, society for a period of years still remained feudal. In the first months of Soviet rule the proletariat reigned on the basis of bourgeois economy. In the field of agriculture the dictatorship of the proletariat operated for a number of years on the basis of petty-bourgeois economy (to a considerable degree it does so even now). Should a bourgeois counterrevolution succeed in Russia, the new government for a lengthy period would have to base itself upon nationalized economy. But what does such a type of temporary conflict between economy and the state mean? It means a *revolution* or a *counterrevolution.* The victory of one class over another signifies that it will reconstruct economy in the interests of the victory. But such a condition of transition appearing during the necessary time in every social revolution, has nothing in common with the theory of a classless state which in the absence of a real boss is being exploited by a clerk, i.e., by the bureaucracy."

This paragraph deserves the closest study and thought, in my opinion, for the light it can shed on the events in Eastern Europe. For one thing, it seems to me to place the question of the class relations in agriculture in their properly subordinate place in determining the character of the state.

More important, it indicates the contradiction that can exist for a time between the economy and state during a transition period. Finally, it reaffirms the Marxist law that a fundamental change in property relations cannot occur without the intrusion of a revolutionary or counterrevolutionary force. The events in Eastern Europe constitute a test of these propositions. The problem is to work out how they either confirm or invalidate Trotsky's theses.

This cannot be done without a thorough understanding of what Trotsky says about the relation between our revolutionary norms and the reality that we must appraise according to scientific criteria.

### Criteria and norms

"It is the substitution of a subjective, 'normative' method for that of an objective, dialectical," Trotsky continues, "which renders it difficult for many comrades to form a correct sociological appraisal of the USSR. Not without reason do Burnham and Carter say that the Soviet Union cannot be considered a workers state 'in the traditional sense given to this term by Marxism.' This simply means that the USSR does not correspond to the norms of a workers state as set forth in our program."

To illustrate his meaning, Trotsky uses the familiar analogy between a workers state and a trade union. Our norm, embodied in the program we fight for, calls for a trade union to be an organization of class struggle. But reality gives a different kind of trade union, in fact a great variety of them. Some of them are definitely reactionary but that doesn't mean they are not trade unions.

Trotsky then tells us by what criteria we can distinguish both trade unions and workers states: "The class character of the state is determined by its relation to the forms of property in the means of production. The character of such a workers organization as that of a trade union is determined by its relation to the distribution of national income." Because William Green & Co. defend private property in the means of production they are bourgeois. So long as the AFL bureaucracy is forced to defend the workers' share of the national income, however, they continue to head genuine trade unions. "This objective symptom is sufficient in all important cases to permit us to draw a line of demarcation between the most reactionary trade union and an organization of scabs."

"The function of Stalin, like the function of Green, has a dual character. Stalin serves the bureaucracy and thus the world bourgeoisie; but he cannot defend the bureaucracy other than by defending that social foundation which the bureaucracy exploits in its own interests. To that extent does Stalin defend nationalized property from imperialist attacks and from the too impatient and avaricious layers of this very bureaucracy. However, he carries through this defense with methods that prepare the general destruction of Soviet society."

Then comes a most interesting observation: "Historical development has accustomed us to the most varied kind of trade unions: militant, reformist, revolutionary, reactionary, liberal, and Catholic. It is otherwise with a workers government. Such a phenomenon we see for the first time. That accounts for our inclination to approach the USSR exclusively from the point of view of the *norms* of the revolutionary program. Meanwhile the workers state is an objective historical *fact* which is being subjected to the influence of different historical forces and can as we see come into full contradiction with 'traditional' norms."

As if anticipating the objection that our norms must be based on reality and consequently are not utopian ideals Trotsky observes, "It is of course necessary not to forget that we expect programmatic norms to be realized only if they are the generalized expression of the progressive tendencies of the *historical process itself.*"

How this works out in practice, Trotsky illustrates as follows: "The programmatic definition of a union would sound approximately like this: an organization of workers of a profession or of an industry with the objective of (1) struggling against capital for the amelioration of the conditions of the workers, (2) participating in the revolutionary struggle for the overthrow of the bourgeoisie, (3) participating in the organization of economy on a socialist basis. If we compared this 'normative' definition with the actual reality, we should find ourselves constrained to say: there is not a single fact, that is to say, of the *generalized* expression of the development to the *particular* manifestation of this same development—such a formal, ultimatistic, non-dialectic counterpoise between program and reality is absolutely lifeless and does not open any road for the intervention of the revolutionary party. In the meantime the actual opportunistic unions under the pressure of capitalist disintegration *can* and under the conditions of our correct policies within the unions, *must* approach our programmatic norms and play a progressive historical role. This, of course, presupposes a complete change in leadership."

If we extend this line of thought to the complicated problem of Eastern Europe will it help us reach a solution? I think it will. Certainly it must be admitted in theory that besides the USSR other particular instances of workers states may deviate from the norm. Trotsky did not live to see the appearance of such new cases, but he showed us how to approach them. Once again, let's see how he utilized the example of the Soviet Union:

"The pressure of imperialism on the Soviet Union has as its aim the alteration of the very nature of Soviet society. The struggle—today peaceful, tomorrow military—concerns the forms of property. In the capacity of a gear wheel in this struggle, the bureaucracy leans now on the proletariat against imperialism, now on imperialism against the proletariat, in order to increase its own authority. (How well have we seen this illustrated in Eastern Europe!—J.H.) At the same time it mercilessly exploits its role as distributor of the meagre wants of life in order to safeguard its own well-being and power. By this token the rule of the proletariat assumes an abridged, curbed, distorted character. One can with full justification say that the proletariat, *ruling* in one backward and isolated country, still remains an *oppressed* class. The source of oppression is world imperialism; the mechanism of transmission of the oppression—the bureaucracy. If in these words: 'a ruling and at the same time an oppressed class' there is a contradiction, then it flows not from the mistakes of thought but from the contradiction in the very situation of the USSR. It is precisely because of this that we reject the theory of socialism in one country.

"The recognition of the USSR as a workers state—not a type but the mutilation of a type—does not at all signify a theoretical and political amnesty for the Soviet bureaucracy. On the contrary, its reactionary character is fully revealed only in the light of the contradiction between its antiproletarian politics and the needs of the workers state. Only by posing the question in this manner does our exposure of the Stalinist clique gain full motive force."

In the light of these instructive remarks of Trotsky are we not justified in asking whether or not in our approach to the class character of the Eastern Europe countries we have not been guilty of trying to force these states to fit our norm of a workers state rather than making an objective appraisal of the overturn in property relations? Isn't that why we hesitate to call them by their right name, "workers states"?

Up to now I have not added any adjective to this category although it is obvious that one is required. I am quite prepared to take any that seems most appropriate, "deformed," "degenerated," "mutilated"—any word that will indicate most clearly that we mean a monstrous and not a normal instance of the type. In the case of the Soviet Union, Trotsky was willing to go even further on the adjective so long as the noun—the basic category—was preserved.

Here is what he says on page 79 of *In Defense of Marxism* [2020 printing]: "Some voices cry out: 'If we continue to recognize the USSR as a workers state, we will have to establish a new category: the counterrevolutionary workers state.' This argument attempts to shock our imagination by opposing a good programmatic norm to a miserable, mean, even repugnant reality. But haven't we observed from day to day since 1923 how the Soviet state has played a more and more counterrevolutionary role on the international arena? Have we forgotten the experience of the Chinese Revolution, of the 1926 general strike in England and finally the very fresh experience of the Spanish revolution? There are two completely counterrevolutionary workers internationals. These critics have apparently forgotten this 'category.' The trade unions of France, Great Britain, the United States and other countries support completely the counterrevolutionary politics of their bourgeoisie. This does not prevent us from labeling them trade unions, from supporting their progressive steps and from defending them against the bourgeoisie. Why is it impossible to employ the same method with the counterrevolutionary workers state? In the last analysis a workers state is a trade union which has conquered power. The difference in attitude in these two cases is explainable by the simple fact that the trade unions have a long history and we have become accustomed to consider them as realities and not simply as 'categories' in our program. But, as regards the workers state there is being evinced an inability to learn to approach it as a real historical fact which has not subordinated itself to our program."

Let us visualize the USSR as a reactionary trade union where the bureaucracy practices racketeering, concludes sell-out agreements with the bosses, strong-arms the membership and rubs out opposition voices wherever they are heard. Is it stretching the analogy too much to visualize the bureaucracy of this union, after overcoming one terrible threat of being crushed and facing another even more dangerous threat, now trying to strengthen the union's position in their own peculiar fashion by organizing what they consider vital territory?

Is it stretching the analogy to consider these bureaucrats so fearful of the introduction of a little democracy and fresh forces—even though they're hungry for the dues—that they are extremely hesitant and fearful about admitting these new locals to full membership and will even use the help of the bosses if necessary to make sure of their bureaucratic grip?

Suppose that some of the membership in these new Eastern European locals rebel against the bureaucrats even though they were trained in the same school of bad unionism and are forced to split. Should it be so difficult for us to determine whether they are genuine unions or not?

Why can't we approach these new formations in Eastern Europe with the same assurance we would if they had been born in a conflict between a union-smashing employers' association and the bureaucracy-ridden Teamsters' Union headed by Tobin instead of a conflict between German imperialism and the USSR headed by Stalin? It seems to me we can if we stick to the old criteria and don't drag in innovations that force us to call them scab outfits and company unions simply because they're small, weak and lack the resources of the giant parent body that gave them the impulse to organize and is now winding them in bureaucratic chains. At the next stage they can provide the spark for a new mighty surge forward, especially if we can find a means of bringing our program to their attention.

### Emphasizing the differences

Before turning to what appears to me to be the correct solution of the problem of Eastern Europe, I want to take up some of the arguments that have been advanced against calling these countries "workers states."

First, the argument that we should emphasize the *differences* between Yugoslavia, say, and the USSR rather than the *similarities*. How this can get us anywhere in determining what kind of state we have before us seems obscure. We can agree to emphasize the differences and still not move ahead an inch.

Emphasizing the differences between a vicious bull dog and a litter of Pekingese pups doesn't help us to determine whether the newly-born animals are misshapen dogs or simply degenerated wolves on the road to structural assimilation with the hungry bull dog. We must still decide on our criteria of what constitutes a dog.

You can list all the similarities and differences between Yugoslavia and the USSR, emphasize one or the other, and still you are faced with the questions: Are these quantitative or qualitative differences? How do you tell the USSR from a capitalist state? How do you tell the class character of Yugoslavia? Do the same criteria apply in both cases? What is the qualitative point of change in determining a reversal in the class character of a state?

Strangely enough, the comrades who insist on our emphasizing the differences between the USSR and Yugoslavia also insist on our emphasizing the *similarities* between Yugoslavia and China. They ask, if Yugoslavia is a workers state, what about China? The truth, however, is concrete. To determine the character of the states in Eastern Europe, each one has to be appraised in its own right. We have to know what has happened to the bourgeoisie, what has happened to property relations. This likewise holds for China where the greatest upheaval since 1917 is occurring. The problem of China fully deserves individual treatment and we need not try to merge it at this stage with the problem of Yugoslavia and so dissolve the concrete in the abstract.

### Dependence on the world market

It is contended that countries like Yugoslavia are far more dependent on the world market than the USSR and consequently cannot be considered workers states. But this does not determine the class character of these countries. It simply shows that they are weaker and far more easily affected by external pressures than the Soviet Union. This fact offers a positive point of approach in advancing our program.

Pertinent to this contention, we should remember that as the USSR advanced, it became more dependent on the world market. This increased the danger to the USSR but did not change its class character.

Trotsky pointed to the growing dependence of the USSR on the world market as another argument against the pernicious theory of socialism in one country. (See *Third International After Lenin,* "The Dependence of the USSR on World Economy," pp. 67–76 [2020 printing].) Trotsky could not convince the majority because the self-sufficiency of the USSR loomed too large at the time.

In the case of countries with a greater degree of dependence on the world market, this task should be easier. We point to the dependence to show how vital it is to win political allies abroad and to advance the program of revolutionary socialism.

This false criterion seems to be derived from our norm calling for an end to dependence on the world market through extending the socialist revolution. It is not, however, one of the classic Trotskyist criteria of a workers state.

### 'Instability'

Another "criterion" advanced is the relative instability of these countries compared to the Soviet Union.

Of course they are more unstable. If they are not absorbed by the USSR or do not succeed in winning their independence, their life span will be incomparably shorter than that of the USSR unless they conduct truly revolutionary politics on the international arena. That opens up possibilities for the growth of Trotskyism in these lands if we are able to penetrate them with our ideas. But the relative instability of these regimes certainly is not a valid criterion in determining their class character. At best it cannot be anything but an indication that something fundamental such as civil war, revolution or counterrevolution, an acute class struggle, is occurring, or that the country is weak relative to the big world powers.

Such considerations seem to have been thrown into the hopper with no thought of their relevance or specific weight but simply on the hunch that they can't do any harm and might do some good. Sheer quantity might produce a qualitative change in the minds of those who have been thinking about calling a country like Yugoslavia a workers state.

### The national boundaries

As the Trotskyist movement has insisted thousands of times, the old national boundaries today are as reactionary as private property in the means of production. Our socialist norm calls for their abolition so that humanity can move forward. But does that mean that Yugoslavia, confined within its narrow national boundaries cannot be characterized for that reason as a workers state?

This is really a corollary of the argument about "real planning" and stands or falls with it. Our norm for building the socialist society calls for "real planning" and you can't have real planning until you do away with the reactionary national boundaries. That's why we call for the abolition of national boundaries as an essential part of the struggle for socialism. But we are faced with the problem of appraising real formations in which we must find a foothold for our norms.

Let's take an example. We call for an independent Soviet Ukraine. Suppose a real movement gets under way and the Ukraine achieves independence under a Soviet regime. The Kremlin of course could never survive the political consequences of such an event. However, in theory it might hang on for a time. Would we then refuse to call the Ukraine a workers state because planning would be hampered by the narrow, stifling national boundaries?

### Objections of a more fundamental character

These objections are not very solid. However, those reluctant to pin the label "workers state" on any of the Eastern European countries have much weightier arguments in their arsenal. These can be placed under three general headings: (1) class relations in production, (2) pillage and distribution of the national income, (3) political consequences to the Trotskyist movement. This is of course only a rough approximation. I make it only in order to underline the fact that arguments coming under these different headings thereby carry different weight.

Of decisive importance are those dealing with the class relations in production. Marxists determine the class nature of a state from the relations in production, not from the forms of distribution (even though the two in the historic sense are reciprocally related) or from the immediate political consequences to revolutionary socialism.

First of all it is necessary to underline once again the facts established by the Plenum resolution: that the "propertied classes in these countries" are "dying"; that the conclusion of the resolution as to the class character of the buffer zone "does not at all imply that the bourgeoisie is in power as the dominant class in these countries."

The liquidation of the bourgeoisie as the dominant class in these countries is the cornerstone of the position that they must be considered workers states. If the bourgeoisie still constituted the ruling class, then nationalization by itself would not make these countries workers states. However, the facts indicate that we must characterize that possibility as an abstraction which does not correspond with the true situation.

If the resolution is wrong in this respect, if the comrades familiar with the facts have not given us an accurate picture, and the bourgeoisie actually still remains the dominant class, then it would be necessary to say that the states are capitalist. But the presentation of the facts about Eastern Europe appears to me to be the strongest side of the resolution.

Besides the displacement of the bourgeoisie as the ruling class, we have the virtually complete conversion of industry, of the banking system, of communications and transport into state-owned property. These are heavy facts and must be given their due weight in any Marxist analysis, for they concern the decisive sphere of class relations in production.

Because it comes in this general sphere, the argument that none of these countries, including Yugoslavia, can be considered "workers states" because they are predominantly agricultural and agriculture has not been nationalized, is in my opinion the strongest argument for calling them "capitalist." It demands careful consideration.

### The question of agriculture

That these countries are predominantly agricultural is most certainly true. However, as we know, agriculture develops much more slowly toward advanced capitalist forms than does industry. Even in the United States, agriculture is far more backward than industry and consequently plays a much less decisive role in the social and political life of the country. If the bourgeoisie is overthrown in a country that is predominantly agricultural, and industry becomes state property, the government replaces the capitalist class as the hub around which the agricultural spokes revolve. Thus the nationalization of the land, important and essential as it is, does not have the same weight as the breaking of bourgeois rule and the nationalization of industry.

In Eastern Europe, to gauge the relative strength of agriculture as compared with industry, we must also know what proportion of agriculture was represented by big capitalist farmers, what proportion by medium capitalist farmers and what proportion by peasants producing primarily for immediate family use, and how powerful the feudal vestiges were when the Red Army moved across these lands. Then we must know the result of the peasant attacks on landed property. What proportion of agriculture today still remains in the hands of feudalistic landlords? Of big capitalist farmers? Of small farmers? Of peasants so poverty-stricken they do not produce primarily on a commodity basis? What is the real relationship of class forces today?

If, for example, the grip of the landlords has been broken, the land redistributed, and the big farms either divided or taken over by the state; if the government is pushing a program of collectivization, then the failure up to now to nationalize the land is less important than the other criteria in this sphere. Under such conditions, command of industry is decisive and to cite merely the proportion of agriculture a country has in general—without differentiating its class composition—can be quite misleading in determining the class character of the state.

In the case of Poland and Finland, Trotsky forecast that in the civil war accompanying the advance of the Red Army at the opening of World War II measures would be taken against the big landholders. He turned out to be right.

Similar action was taken against the big landholders after the war in Eastern Europe. The caution and delay exercised by the Stalinists in this field in going further could be ascribed to an effort to win the small peasants or at least neutralize them—to give them guarantees for the time being. Such guarantees can always be taken away, since legal documents are only scraps of paper to the Stalinists. In agriculture as in so many other fields, it is necessary to go by specific actions and not by the official pronouncements of Stalinist "program," important as they are from a different point of view.

An additional observation should be made at this point. In our desire to solve the problem of the character of the Eastern Europe countries we should not overlook our own political problems here at home. One of the problems we have yet to work out in detail is how to win the active sympathy of the farmers.

The main line is given in our Transition Program, but it is only a beginning: "The program for the *nationalization of the land and collectivization of agriculture* should be so drawn that from its very basis it should exclude the possibility of expropriation of small farmers and their compulsory collectivization. The farmer will remain owner of his plot of land as long as he himself believes it possible or necessary. In order to rehabilitate the program of socialism in the eyes of the farmer, it is necessary to expose mercilessly the Stalinist methods of collectivization which are dictated not by the interests of the farmers or workers but by the interests of the bureaucracy." (Leon Trotsky, *The Transitional Program for Socialist Revolution*, p. 165 [2020 printing].)

This gives us a good hint of how far back we must lean in this question for *political* reasons. Note in passing how the bourgeois democratic task, "nationalization of the land," is combined with the socialist task, "collectivization of agriculture."

The Transition Program continues: "The expropriation of the expropriators likewise does not signify forcible confiscation of the property of artisans and shopkeepers. On the contrary, workers control of banks and trusts—even more, the nationalization of these concerns—can create for the urban petty bourgeoisie incomparably more favorable conditions of credit, purchase, and sale than is possible under the unchecked domination of the monopolies. Dependence upon private capital will be replaced by dependence upon the State, which will be the more attentive to the needs of its small coworkers and agents the stronger the toilers themselves will keep control of the State in their hands.

"The practical participation of the exploited farmers in the control of different fields of economy will allow them to decide for themselves whether or not it would be profitable for them to go over to collective working of the land—at what date and on what scale. Industrial workers should consider themselves duty bound to show farmers every cooperation in traveling this road: through the trade unions, factory committees, and, most important, through a workers and farmers government."

One of the biggest crimes of Stalinism has been to forcibly expropriate small farmers and businessmen against their will. We have to "rehabilitate the program of socialism in the eyes of the farmer."

This attitude toward the petty bourgeoisie is not motivated *primarily* by political considerations, although it is obvious what weight they have. The tactic is based on much deeper grounds.

As Lenin explained, "Theoretically, nationalization is the 'ideally' pure development of capitalism in agriculture." (See "The Agrarian Program of the Social-Democracy in the First Russian Revolution, 1905–1907," in Lenin, *Collected Works*, vol. 13, pp. 217–431.) Lenin pointed out that nationalization of the land could speed the development of capitalist relations in agriculture. The bourgeoisie, however, never nationalized the land in any of their revolutions against feudalism. They did not do so because (1) they did not carry out their historic tasks to their logical conclusion; (2) on the appearance of the working class as an independent force in society they compromised with feudalistic reaction, permitting certain of its forms of exploitation to remain as vestiges. This extra burden on society was entailed by capitalist fear of the proletariat.

Because the bourgeoisie is no longer capable of carrying out this democratic task where it is required, the workers state has fallen heir to the job. But the workers state undertakes nationalization of the land not to speed the development of capitalist relations in agriculture but to move forward to socialization of agriculture, which is *its* goal.

With the expropriation of the bourgeoisie and the conversion of industry into state-owned property, a force of completely different order than the capitalist class becomes master of society. At first sight it might seem all the more necessary for the workers state—because it is more advanced—to display utter ruthlessness with all these vestiges of the long outmoded past. But we have a qualitatively different relationship from that which existed between capitalism and the feudal remnants that survived under its rule. It is sufficient at first to expropriate the big landlords intimately interlinked with the big capitalists. This leaves the small farmers, shopkeepers and artisans—the classes, which, "no matter how numerically strong they may be, essentially are representative survivals of precapitalist forms of production." *(The Transitional Program for Socialist Revolution*, p. 164.)

As the workers state, particularly in a highly industrialized country like the United States, unfolds its dynamic power, the danger of a rebirth of capitalism from the petty bourgeoisie reaches the vanishing point. Even though the workers state offers them better opportunities for a good living than capitalism while still permitting them to continue their habitual mode of life, the socialist opportunities opening up on every hand are so much more attractive that most of them of their own free volition will give up the dead past and join in the great work of pioneering the new society. Those incapable of making the change need not be molested. The younger generation, freed from the stifling, fear-ridden atmosphere of capitalism, will grow up with new horizons and completely different concepts of what constitutes the best way to live.

These considerations compel us to say that nationalization of the land, with all that it entails, must be viewed in a somewhat different light than nationalization of industries expropriated from the bourgeoisie in determining the class character of the state.

### Does pillage determine the character of a state?

Let us now turn to the important but less weighty arguments concerning pillage and the distribution of national income.

"In view of the pillage inflicted on the Eastern European countries," it is asked, "are we not obliged to call them 'capitalist'?"

If a gangster holds up a worker, takes his pay envelope, his weekend sack of groceries, his shirt, pants, shoes and streetcar fare and gives him a kick down the street, are we obliged to call the worker a gangster too?

We determine what class the worker belongs to by his relation in the factory to the capitalist class and not by the assorted loan sharks, trade union bureaucrats, strong-arm artists and other parasites who victimize him.

As Trotsky said of the Kremlin vermin: "To put it plainly, insofar as the bureaucracy robs the people (and this is done in various ways by every bureaucracy), we have to deal not with *class exploitation*, in the scientific sense of the word, but with *social parasitism,* although on a very large scale." (*Writings [1933–34]*, p. 151.)

Our opponents rejoin: "But what about the recognition of foreign debts and the compensation in some instances to foreign capitalists whose holdings were nationalized?"

We will not ask how much the foreign capitalists have realized or expect to realize from the Stalinist recognition of these imperialist financial demands. Actual payment will in all probability depend on the international relationship of forces and how essential it is to the Stalinists and the Tito regime to meet the price demanded by the imperialist bandits for essential goods. Like other international "debts" owed by European countries, they have been "recognized." Yet if they are never paid it will not violate the European tradition.

Even if they are forced to pay this foreign tribute, however, it does not make these countries capitalist.

"You forget the exploitation imposed on the Eastern European countries by the Kremlin through mixed companies and other means. Doesn't this exploitation oblige us to call them 'capitalist'?"

Yes, it does—if you consider the USSR to be capitalist and the "buffer zone" to be a colonial area where this capitalist USSR is practicing imperialist exploitation. However, if you still consider the USSR to be a degenerated workers state, it does not seem quite accurate to me to call this form of pillage "capitalist exploitation." The "exploitation" conducted by the USSR in Eastern Europe is symmetrical to imperialist exploitation just as the police regime in the USSR is symmetrical to a fascist regime. But the two are not identical. Just as pillage does not necessarily make the victim "capitalist," so it does not necessarily make those who practice it "capitalist."

Comes the inevitable outcry: "You want us to settle for these revolting formations as 'workers states'! You call into question the whole idea of emancipating humanity from the filth and decay of capitalism through the workers state. The whole point of a workers state is that the workers create a new type structure in which the most essential item is the participation of the workers themselves in the government. Where does this exist in Eastern Europe?"

Our sympathy is wholly with the comrades who feel this way about it. We too would have felt much happier if history had seen fit right now to give us another example of a model workers state, such as the Soviet Union under Lenin and Trotsky, instead of these deformed offspring of the degenerated workers state. What can we say except that Stalinism continues to befoul the name of communism and everything associated with it? What can we do but continue the onerous task of trying to clean out this Augean stable? To succeed in this, and especially to help the workers and poor farmers in Eastern Europe develop a powerful opposition movement to Stalinism, demands first of all clarity in theory and a precise scientific accounting of what has happened in these lands. If you can't smell violets don't blame us. We have only a theoretical fork to work with and not a revolutionary river like Hercules.

As for the argument itself, let us recall Trotsky's answer to the same argument applied to the USSR: "Where and in what books can one find a faultless prescription for a proletarian dictatorship? The dictatorship of a class does not mean by a long shot that its entire mass always participates in the management of the state. This we have seen, first of all, in the case of the propertied classes. The nobility ruled through the monarchy before which the noble stood on his knees. The dictatorship of the bourgeoisie took on comparatively developed democratic forms only under the conditions of capitalist upswing when the ruling class had nothing to fear." Trotsky then cites the example of Germany where the bourgeoisie still ruled although "politically it is placed under complete subjection to Hitler and his bands." Despite Hitler's political dictatorship, "the dictatorship of the bourgeoisie remains inviolate in Germany, because all the conditions of its social hegemony have been preserved and strengthened. By expropriating the bourgeoisie politically Hitler saved it, even if temporarily, from economic expropriation."

Examples like this, used by Trotsky, should be studied. They contain the key to understanding the Stalinist role not only in the USSR but in those areas where it extends its rule and overturns property relations.

"Anticipating our subsequent arguments," Trotsky continues, "our opponents will hasten to refute: although the bourgeoisie, as an exploiting minority can also preserve its hegemony by means of a fascist dictatorship, the proletariat building a socialist society must manage its government itself, directly drawing ever wider masses of the people into the task of government. In its general form, this argument is undebatable, but in the *given* case it merely means that the present Soviet dictatorship is a sick dictatorship." (*Writings* [1933–34], pp. 137–38.)

### Trotsky on Poland and Finland

Although it cannot be decisive in a scientific analysis, one of the arguments raised against our position that demands most thoughtful evaluation is the contention that it implies revision of the Marxist theory of the state. It is held that we leave the door open to the possibility that the class character of the state can be changed by manipulation from the top, by "cold" means. This in turn implies, it is contended, a concession to Stalinism and even to Social Democratic revisionism—to Stalinism because it would then have a historic future; to Social Democratic revisionism because its theory of achieving socialism through manipulation of capitalist government posts would then turn out to be correct. In that case, what perspective remains open to the Fourth International?

If we are to talk of revision, I think that the comrades who support the Plenum resolution should first make sure there are no flaws in their position. A shift has been made on this question as can be seen from the differences between the theses of the World Congress which say that the destruction of capitalism is "impossible" without the revolutionary mobilization of the masses and the Plenum resolution which explains how the bourgeoisie were ousted as the ruling class in the Eastern European countries by "cold" means.

My own impression is that the resolution concedes too much. It brings into question the Marxist theory of the state unless abstract references to the domestic and world relationship of forces can satisfy you as an adequate explanation of the apparent violation of the laws of the class struggle.

To find our way out of this trap it may be helpful to turn again to Trotsky's writings on Poland and Finland and refresh our memories on how he approached the same general problem. First of all on the importance of the Kremlin's actions in these territories for our appraisal of the USSR:

"Let us for a moment conceive that in accordance with the treaty with Hitler, the Moscow government leaves untouched the rights of private property in the occupied areas and limits itself to 'control' after the fascist pattern. Such a concession would have a deep-going principled character and might become a starting point for a new appraisal on our part of the nature of the Soviet state." (*In Defense of Marxism*, p. 68.)

This is a most important consideration for us today. If the rights of private property have been left inviolate in the occupied territories, as some comrades think, and the Moscow government really has the perspective of limiting itself to "control" after the fascist pattern or in the "capitalist" way, it becomes our duty to begin thinking of a new appraisal of the character of the USSR.

In 1939, however, Trotsky foresaw the more probable variant. Instead of limiting itself to "control" of "private property in the occupied areas," said Trotsky, "It is more likely . . . that in the territories scheduled to become a part of the USSR, the Moscow government will carry through the expropriation of the large landowners and statification of the means of production. This variant is most probable not because the bureaucracy remains true to the socialist program but because it is neither desirous nor capable of sharing the power, and the privileges the latter entails, with the old ruling classes in the occupied territories."

Isn't this an accurate forecast of the events in Eastern Europe in the post-war period? Trotsky continues:

"Here an analogy literally offers itself. The first Bonaparte halted the revolution by means of a military dictatorship. However, when the French troops invaded Poland, Napoleon signed a decree: 'Serfdom is abolished.' This measure was dictated not by Napoleon's sympathies for the peasants, nor by democratic principles, but rather by the fact that the Bonapartist dictatorship based itself not on feudal, but on bourgeois property relations. Inasmuch as Stalin's Bonapartist dictatorship bases itself not on private but on state property, the invasion of Poland by the Red Army should, in the nature of the case, result in the abolition of private capitalist property, so as thus to bring the regime of the occupied territories into accord with the regime of the USSR." (*In Defense of Marxism*, pp. 68–69)

This fruitful analogy could well be developed it appears to me for publication in *Fourth International*. A study of the similarities between the consequences of the advance of Napoleon's armies and those of Stalin's armies would be of absorbing interest for the light it would cast on what is happening today in Eastern Europe.

To continue with Trotsky's remarks: "This measure, revolutionary in character—'the expropriation of the expropriators'—is in this case achieved in a military-bureaucratic fashion. The appeal to independent activity on the part of the masses in the new territories—and without such an appeal, even if worded with extreme caution it is impossible to constitute a new regime—will on the morrow undoubtedly be suppressed by ruthless police measures in order to assure the preponderance of the bureaucracy over the awakened revolutionary masses."

Trotsky followed with the minutest attention the impulse the approach of the Red Army gave to the masses of Poland. He characterized what happened as "civil war." It is obvious why he did. Overturns in property relations cannot occur without the revolutionary mobilization of the masses. Consequently he was keenly interested in how the facts forecast by Marxist law would turn out and how far they would deviate, under the influence of Stalinism, from our programmatic norms for a revolutionary mobilization of the masses.

Again in Finland, Trotsky watched for similar manifestations. There even such symptoms as brother fighting brother were taken by him as manifestations of "civil war."

In an article for the *St. Louis Post-Dispatch*, written in January 1940, Trotsky explained: "In order to include Finland in the framework of the USSR—and such is now the obvious aim of the Kremlin—it is necessary to sovietize her, i.e., carry through an expropriation of the higher layer of landowners and capitalists. To accomplish such a revolution in the relations of property is impossible without a civil war. The Kremlin will do everything in order to attract to its side the Finnish industrial workers and the lower stratum of the farmers. Once the Moscow oligarchy finds itself compelled to play with the fire of war and revolution, it will try at least to warm its hands. It will undoubtedly achieve certain successes in this way." (*Fourth International*, August 1942, p. 254.)

Observe that Trotsky does not refer to "real planning." He calls the expropriation of the *higher layer* of landowners and capitalists a "revolution in the relations of property." Observe too that Trotsky did not expect civil war in its classic form. "Warm its hands," he said of Moscow's playing with the fire of war and revolution.

Speaking more specifically of the civil war in his "Open Letter to Burnham," Trotsky said: "Naturally, this is a civil war of a special type. It does not arise spontaneously from the depths of the popular masses. It is not conducted under the leadership of the Finnish revolutionary party based on mass support. It is introduced on bayonets from without. It is controlled by the Moscow bureaucracy." (*In Defense of Marxism*, p. 172.) In other words, this civil war departs widely from our "norms" but nevertheless the fact that a civil war is occurring must be recognized.

Trotsky visualized two stages in the Soviet advance. The first one was the stage of the "deformed," "distorted" or, to use Trotsky's phrase, "special type" civil war. The second stage, he warned, would be the swift political strangulation of the movement by the Moscow bureaucracy when it established its totalitarian rule in the new areas. In a letter, Trotsky wrote: "It is not necessary to repeat that the civil war in Finland as was the case in Poland would have a limited, semi-stifled nature and that it can, in the next stage, go over into a civil war between the Finnish masses and the Moscow bureaucracy. We know this at least as clearly as the opposition and we openly warn the masses. But we analyze the process as it is and we don't identify the first stage with the second one." (*In Defense of Marxism*, p. 147.) We can add also that Trotsky didn't demand that the civil war meet his norms, which as everyone knows were of the highest, before he would consent to characterize it as civil war, even if of a "special type."

If you study Trotsky's writings of this period closely, you cannot help being struck at how well his analysis of the Polish and Finnish events anticipated what happened when the Soviet forces moved westward against the German imperialist armies. This follows from the fact that Trotsky's analysis was not simply an analysis after the event, it was a *prognosis* of what would happen upon the expansion of the degenerated workers state under Stalinist domination.

There was the first stage, far more distinct than in 1939–40, of civil war. What had been attempted in 1939–40 under the contemptuous gaze of Hitler and then interrupted by the most frightful war in history, was now resumed on the heels of the retreating German armies and in face of the colossal defeat of the Nazi regime. This stage was more distinct because the uprisings were more spontaneous, welling from much deeper roots and a wider base. After all, the masses were responding to the advance of a *victorious* Red Army, a Red Army victorious over the Nazi military machine, and not one that had been mauled by the small Finnish forces. That was a tremendous new fact. The Kremlin didn't need to issue appeals to the masses as in the pre-war situation. It was faced with a different problem. How to keep the masses in hand? In many instances, the peasants finished off the big landlords. The workers in many factories formed committees to take over.

Stage two came fast, the political crackdown. The unbridled character of this crackdown was a measure of the depth of the revolutionary impulse touched off by the advance of the Red Army. That impulse frightened the Kremlin. This was fire that could spread with lightning speed. That was why they utilized sections of the bourgeoisie, particularly their political representatives and functionaries, to bring the political whip down on the face of the masses. The political danger arising from the revolutionary impulse impressed the Kremlin far more than the political, economic and military danger from the enfeebled bourgeoisie bowing and scraping before the bayonets of the eastern conqueror.

Protected by the guns of the Red Army, the Stalinists took key positions in the civil bureaucracy and the armed forces, paying special attention to the armed forces, which in conditions of civil war, no matter how attenuated, play a more decisive role than the civil bureaucracy which is normally in control. We can see how this works out almost any week in the Latin American countries when those in control of the armed forces topple the civil regime. Having got the political bridle on the masses, the Stalinists then turned against the remnants of the bourgeoisie and their political agents which they had previously used against the proletariat and began the process of shattering their remaining positions.

One cannot help recalling how the relatively strong bourgeoisie in Western Europe used the Stalinists at the end of the war to stave off revolution, gain time, strengthen their political positions with the help of American military and economic might and then tossed the Stalinist officials like squeezed lemons into the garbage pail. In Eastern Europe, with the help of Russian arms and the GPU, the Stalinists were sufficiently strong to reverse this general tactic on the political field, using bourgeois agents to help entrench their own bureaucratic regime and then discarding or absorbing them. This stage was more or less combined with the acceleration and extension of nationalization.

The Stalinists even mobilized the workers against the bourgeoisie where they felt sufficiently sure of keeping the action under control. Paul G. Stevens, reporting in the March 1, 1948 *Militant* on the Stalinist use of "Action Committees" in Czechoslovakia, says: "The Stalinists, in accordance with the new Cominform line, are apparently trying to use mass action in order to align Czechoslovakia with Moscow as completely as the rest of Eastern Europe.

"While the Stalinist leaders are basing themselves on mass action, they are proceeding with a caution that reveals their fear of its revolutionary impulse."

To be sure, Comrade Stevens apparently does not believe that this constitutes genuine civil war since he continues: "Should a civil war actually erupt, the likelihood is that the situation will grow out of hand, no matter what the bureaucratic plans." And this estimate is quite correct if by "civil war" you mean an action that corresponds with our norms. Looked at objectively, however, wherein did this action differ from the actions seen in Poland and Finland when the Kremlin moved, or tried to move, forward?

Because of the extreme enfeeblement of the native bourgeoisie, the inability of either German or Allied imperialism to come to their rescue, and the profound desire of the masses to rid themselves at any cost of the strangling yoke of capitalism, it did not take much more civil war to dispose of this "lumpen-bourgeoisie," as Comrade Stevens once aptly termed them, than you can get out of a good Flit gun. Still it must be characterized as "civil war."

Now, if we do not draw air-tight, metaphysical dividing lines between the various stages of this process in Eastern Europe, but for theoretical purposes consider it as a whole; that is, regard this entire period since the Red Army entered these fringe-lands of the USSR in combat with the German armies as one "moment," an episode in world history, what is it but a social revolution started by the masses under the influence of the Soviet Union and deformed by the political counterrevolution conducted by the Kremlin?

Thus everything is accounted for according to the laws of the class struggle as developed by the founders of Marxism. All we had to do was apply some of Trotsky's teachings and not let our norms of planning and civil war interfere with our appraisal of reality. It appears to me that what has been happening in Eastern Europe offers the most brilliant confirmation of the correctness of Trotsky's analysis and prognosis in 1939–40 and confirms what he taught about the character of the state. What other state in the world could have given the impulse to the events we see today in Eastern Europe in the peculiar form they have taken except the degenerated workers state? You can trace not only the obvious stamp of the rapacious bureaucracy but even the mark of the mutilated, desecrated October Revolution serving notice that it is still alive and carries burning coals.

### Our political perspective

Will Stalin now withdraw from these countries? The Kremlin is capable of anything. If it could get a sufficiently favorable deal from Washington it might do what it could to help liquidate the steps taken so far or at least retire while Western imperialism tried to do what it did in Greece. But will Washington give such a deal or does the Kremlin expect such an offer? What guarantees can Washington give that would satisfy the Kremlin sufficiently so that it would dare relinquish its grip on Eastern Europe? Will Washington give up the atom bomb? Its colossal preparations for war? What power politician expects American imperialism to clip its own wings and claws?

The perspective of the Kremlin, if it can be judged correctly from the trend visible in Eastern Europe, is to convert these countries into replicas of the republics in the Soviet Union and to either include them officially in the USSR or to absorb them in effect into the economic framework of the Soviet Union while leaving them formally independent.

No one can mistake Stalin's political perspective. It is to crush all signs of the slightest resistance or potential resistance to this course.

Our political perspective must be based on the widespread opposition to Stalinism among workers and poor farmers and the possibility of its breaking out into the open as in Yugoslavia. This appears to me the most realistic political course. That means, against a bourgeois restoration we defend whatever progressive measures have been taken; against the Kremlin we fight for a genuinely independent Soviet Poland, Soviet Czechoslovakia, etc., on the road toward a Soviet Balkan-Danubian Federation.

Our course should be based on the perspective of Independent Socialist Republics, and if you want the slogan to develop its full potentialities, that means independent of Moscow-directed planning too. Can there be any doubt that Stalin will mobilize every force possible to smash such Republics, to nip any movements in that direction in the bud and to mobilize all possible resources of the planned economy at his disposal to accomplish this counterrevolutionary aim? We have the Kremlin's actions in the case of Yugoslavia. The price of assimilation, of planning organically linked with Moscow's, is abject dependence.

The greatest effectiveness can be given our propaganda if we can point to the truth—that Stalin will stop at nothing, even the liquidation of a workers state, to stay in power. The case of Yugoslavia, explained in these terms, would put an exceedingly sharp edge to our political struggle against Stalinism. As Trotsky said of the USSR, "Only by posing the question in this manner does our exposure of the crimes of the Stalinist clique gain full motive force."

I think this makes clear too that our position offers no comfort to Stalinism. In fact, if we base ourselves on the possibility of new opposition movements arising in Eastern Europe, this position should strengthen our case against Stalinism. We show why the Kremlin moved forward as it did, undermining the defenses of the USSR in its reaction to world imperialism and still worse dealing catastrophic setbacks to the revolutionary socialist movement abroad.

Our analysis of the events in Eastern Europe merely points out the positive side of a development that was a major blow to the socialist movement. While the borderlands experienced an upset in property relations, Stalin's henchmen in France and Italy were knifing workers' uprisings in the back. All Europe, including Germany, might have been socialist today were it not for the crimes of Stalinism at the close of the war. Measured against such blows to the world revolution, the progressive steps in Eastern Europe recede into insignificance.

**Can it be repeated in Western Europe?**

Stalinism cannot repeat in the industrially advanced countries what it did in the backward Eastern European countries. The Western bourgeoisie is too strong. They can get direct help from the arsenals of the United States. They cannot be overthrown without a revolutionary mobilization of the masses that coincides very closely to the "norms" of the Marxist movement.

The events in Eastern Europe do not at all indicate a prolonged lease on life for Stalinism. The whole development constitutes only a brief interlude in history. As Trotsky often said to us, talking about the perspective facing Stalinism in relation to our efforts to save him from assassination, "The wolf is most dangerous in his death agony." By this analogy drawn from his hunting experience in Russia, Trotsky meant that precisely when Stalinism faced its debacle, it could give not only the illusion of greatest strength but even deliver some of its most terrible blows.

In the rebellion of Yugoslavia, the Kremlin sees the handwriting on the wall. The war merely postponed the denouement as war does with all such processes only to speed them up later by way of historic compensation. Stalinism will commit new monstrous crimes against the struggle for socialism, but precisely in Eastern Europe where it has given the appearance of greatest strength, the threads of the monolithic pattern can begin unravelling.

Military-bureaucratic action, which operates in civil war like a flame thrower against isolated detachments, can work only in those specific areas where the bourgeoisie was enfeebled by the war, cut off from the masses, abandoned by its traditional imperialist protectors, subjected to the constrictor-like squeeze of the occupation troops of the Kremlin, and where the masses themselves had illusions at first about Stalinism and the advanced sectors were under its influence.

These concrete conditions do not hold in the West. "But what if the Red Army sweeps to the Atlantic, what then?"

If the Red Army sweeps even to the Adriatic, the curtain may well rise on World War III. It would most certainly signal the opening of World War III if the Kremlin actually lost all contact with reality and undertook the military adventure of plunging forward to the Atlantic. They will hardly be that stupid. The whole course of Stalinism from the beginning has been to try to avoid war (but by means that actually help facilitate the outbreak of war). The bureaucracy has not changed in this respect. Its fear of war has not decreased after the experience of the German invasion and its basic political attitude toward meeting the threat has not changed.

Consequently a westward march of the Red Army would occur only within the frame of an attack initiated by American imperialism.

Aside from the purely military aspect of the question, an overriding political consideration prevents the Kremlin from moving forward. What happened in Yugoslavia is only a mild sample of the reaction that could be expected in Western Germany, France, Italy, Great Britain or the other highly industrialized Western European countries where great masses of workers are rooted in the old cultural centers. The Kremlin knows this. You can imagine what nightmares the Stalinist bureaucrats suffer over small but highly industrialized Czechoslovakia, not to speak of politically awakened Yugoslavia. Their hesitation in moving forward even in Eastern Europe would be multiplied a thousandfold in the cosmopolitan centers of the West. What would result from fraternization between the Red Army and the workers of France! Better let well enough alone.

I repeat, a concrete analysis of the contradictory events in Eastern Europe cannot offer Stalinism any comfort. It can only help in destroying the illusions that the overturn in property relations in Eastern Europe is bound to foster no matter what label you put on these countries.

Labelling such a country in Eastern Europe as Yugoslavia a "workers state" concedes nothing to Stalinism and does not involve a revision of the Marxist theory of the state. On the contrary, it sharpens our attack on Stalinism and is in strict accord with the Marxist theory of the state.

### Can the film be reversed?

It is argued that things can be reversed in these countries and the film wound back to a capitalist restoration without a civil war. This contention seems to me to bring in question the Marxist theory of the state. How can you have a counterrevolution and the restoration of bourgeois property rights without a civil war? You might contend that it would be a peculiar type of civil war, but still it would be a civil war.

The events in Greece, bloody as they were, would be eclipsed by the civil wars that would break out in these countries if a restoration were attempted. The contention that the film can be reversed without a civil war simply follows logically from the thesis that these countries are still capitalist in character. The real situation appears to me quite at variance with this thesis.

Connected with this is the problem of defending the relative gains that have been made in these countries. In the theses of the World Congress, adopted in 1948, a defeatist position is called for in all these lands in the event of war. The Plenum resolution of a year later refers to this position and declares that it still holds good. It adds that we could reconsider this defeatist position only in the event that a qualitative change occurs in the character of their economies. The qualitative change can occur only if "real planning" is introduced. "Real planning" can be introduced only if these states are incorporated in the USSR or in a Balkan-Danube Federation—provided that the Balkan-Danube Federation "forms a genuine unified framework for economic planning."

Consequently it might well turn out that we will become defensists of a Rumania incorporated in the USSR, but defeatists in an independent Yugoslavia. This seems to me an unnecessarily severe penalty for Yugoslavia's inability to meet our norm on "real planning" because of its struggle for independence. Certainly this position stands in the way of the most effective intervention in the Tito-Stalin conflict. Why should we be defensists of the USSR and not of Yugoslavia? It seems to me not only highly advisable politically but also correct in theory.

### The key to the solution

We are faced with an extremely complicated and very difficult problem that requires all our combined efforts for solution. The political side of the problem is to meet the growth in prestige that will accrue to Stalinism through this undeniable overturn in property relations. The theoretical side is to demonstrate how the Marxist laws of the class struggle are once again validated through the developments in Eastern Europe and why they therefore apply in full force, so to speak, or very close to our "norms" in a country like the United States.

The key to the solution of this problem can be found, in my opinion, in Trotsky's handling of the Finnish and Polish events at the opening of the war. He demonstrated how the Marxist law that you cannot have an overturn in property relations without revolution was exemplified in these specific instances.

The law did not come even close in its expression to the "norm" sought by the revolutionary socialist movement. A strong perturbation gave it a pinched, scanty, mutilated, deformed expression. That perturbation came from the Soviet Union, the same source that gave the impulse to the overturn in property relations. Both the source of the perturbation and the source of the impulse can be distinguished. The one was the Stalinist bureaucracy, the other the property relations still remaining from the October Revolution. But the very perturbation, the muffled, strangled form of the law's expression all the more brilliantly demonstrates the operation of that law.

This solution of the central problem, hinging on the origin of the Eastern European countries, seems to me to be the correct one.

### Yugoslavia and the other countries

Some of the comrades who originally considered Yugoslavia to still be a capitalist state are becoming increasingly convinced upon further study and thought that this is an untenable position and that a change will have to be made. They insist, however, that if we are forced to make an exception in the case of Yugoslavia, nevertheless the other Eastern European countries must still be considered as capitalist. To reach this conclusion they utilize the method of "emphasizing the differences" between these countries and Yugoslavia.

This method, I think is not too fruitful. It didn't work very well in the case of Yugoslavia. There, in the attempt to emphasize the differences with the Soviet Union, the Plenum resolution had to bring forward a new criterion, "real planning." Even though it was admitted that "real planning" doesn't exist in the USSR, still a qualitative difference was insisted upon between that planning and the planning you have in Yugoslavia. The criterion that is now advanced as decisive in emphasizing the differences between Yugoslavia and the other Eastern European countries is the occurrence of a "real civil war."

It might well be argued that what occurred in Yugoslavia departs considerably from what should properly be considered a "real civil war." I mention this not to emphasize that difference but merely to show the parallel between the arguments about "real planning" and "real civil war." They are completely symmetrical. What has happened is simply a shift in criteria. "Real planning" is dropped, which permits us to consider Yugoslavia a deformed or mutilated workers state, while the criterion of "real civil war" is advanced, in the absence of which the other countries are automatically barred from being characterized as deformed or mutilated workers states. This, of course, is an easy solution of the difficult problem facing us. But is it correct?

Let us examine again the principal positions in the discussion.

(1) I will take advantage of the opportunity to list my own position first, although as will be seen, there is also a certain logic to the order. In my opinion, in a country where *the rule of the bourgeoisie as a class has been broken* AND *the principle sectors of the economy nationalized* we must place the state in the general category of "workers state" no matter how widely or monstrously it departs from our norms. This change *cannot* occur without a civil war although this civil war may also be a mutilation of the type, differing in important respects from our norms. In Eastern Europe each country must be considered separately to see whether it *in fact* meets these criteria.

(2) The position of those who consider Yugoslavia a workers state but will not admit any of the other Eastern European countries to this category. These comrades agree that destruction of the bourgeoisie and the nationalization of the key sectors of the economy can be taken as decisive criteria provided they are accompanied by a "real civil war." In other words, they either deny that civil war has occurred in the other countries or insist that it does not come up to our specifications. The weakness in their position is to hold that the bourgeoisie can be driven from power and the decisive sectors of the economy nationalized without civil war. They thereby leave the central problem of Eastern Europe still unsolved. The mistake here, it appears to me, is to insist on measuring our norm of civil war against the miserable reality and to refuse to recognize that reality because it is so mangled and distorted.

(3) The position of those who deny that any of the Eastern European countries are workers states. Their decisive criterion is either "real planning" or a vague weighing of "all" the factors and finding that either the decisive one of "real planning" or the overall bundle does not come up to the standard of Marxist norms. The mistake again is insisting that reality come up to our specifications or suffer the penalty of not being recognized for what it is.

(4) The position of those who hold that either in particular or in general not only do the Eastern European countries fail to correspond with our norms but likewise the Soviet Union fails to correspond and that both the USSR and its satellites must for that reason be denied the label "workers state" and called "capitalist" although admittedly an entirely new type of capitalism.

(5) The position of those who hold that the phenomena in the USSR and Eastern Europe depart so far from the norms for both capitalist and workers states that we must call them a completely new type like "bureaucratic collectivism."

At the bottom of each of these positions and modifications of them is lodged a variation in the handling of our norms in relation to reality. Thus we reach the problem of methodology. What is the correct method of relating norms and criteria to concrete events? That question has already been answered. It was answered by Trotsky in the long discussion over the character of the USSR and its first ventures into Eastern Europe. That is one more reason why Trotsky's teachings on these questions are so valuable for our discussion today.

I will conclude by emphasizing the importance of approaching this problem as a collective one. It would be a mistake this early in the discussion to take a hard and fast position and refuse to listen with the greatest attention and open-mindedness to every consideration advanced by those seriously trying to help find the correct solution. Our task is to think things through to the end and to try to contribute what we can to the collective effort to solve the difficult problem of Eastern Europe. If we go about it calmly and with the understanding that this is not a faction fight but a loyal, comradely discussion, I am confident we will succeed.

DECEMBER 1949

# THE KREMLIN'S SATELLITE STATES IN EASTERN EUROPE, YUGOSLAVIA, MARXIST THEORY, AND OUR PERSPECTIVES

By E.R. Frank [BERT COCHRAN]

We are all acquainted with Trotsky's book *Revolution Betrayed,* where he discussed the perspectives for Stalinism as he saw them prior to the outbreak of the war. Trotsky envisaged one way or another the destruction of Stalinism in the course of the war. In the event of victorious socialist revolution, the forces would be set in motion for the undoing of Stalinism in a progressive manner. If the other variant occurred, and capitalism was victorious, the Soviet Union would be defeated, capitalist counterrevolution would triumph in the USSR, and Stalinism would disappear as a world force having lost its state base in the USSR.

We know that due to a peculiar turn of developments, the Kremlin was able to effect an alliance with one group of imperialists against another, and instead of being eliminated from the scene, has succeeded in coming out of the war as the second world power.

While its victory over Nazism inspired the working masses the world over and gave profound impulses to revolutionary actions and uprisings, the victory likewise strengthened world Stalinism and the Kremlin power for the time being, enabled it to stamp out revolutionary manifestations in different parts of the globe and suppress the initiative and straitjacket the independent movements of the proletariat. Furthermore, having emerged as the second world power concomitant with the pulverization of a number of once-powerful imperialist states and the enfeeblement of the bourgeoisie in great sections of the globe, the Kremlin was able to step into these "vacuums," and fasten its sovereignty on great stretches of country, to an extent that none of us had envisaged before the war. These are big new facts of the world situation. Properly analyzed and understood, they point to an extreme weakening of the world imperialist structure, to the beginning of the centrifugal dissolution of Stalinism; they constitute new sources of optimism and open up new perspectives for the world revolution and for our movement. But they must be properly analyzed and understood, else they can lead simply to an angry rejection of important new developments because these do not yet conform to our programmatic demands; the end result of which can be a turning of one's back on the historic process itself.

The discussion of the class nature of the satellite East European states and of Yugoslavia has importance from two points of view. First, the preservation of the internal logic and thought-out character of our theory. We cannot permit our world program to become a "thing of rags and patches," with one set of criteria for the USSR, another set for Eastern Europe, and a third and entirely different set of arguments developed—judging by the ingenuity displayed by some comrades in the present discussion—for the Far East or elsewhere. Second, we must be able to view and analyze great revolutionary mass movements, or even, as in the case of the satellite states in Eastern Europe, important social happenings, without prejudice, even though they are not yet occurring under the leadership of either our program or our movement, and find in them sources of optimism for our future and inspiration for our ranks, rather than embarrassment or discouragement.

The 1949 IEC resolution, while commendable in its summary description of the evolution of the

Reprinted from SWP *Discussion Bulletin,* No. 1, April 1950.

buffer countries, erred in artificially attempting to squeeze them into the Procrustean mold of capitalism, to accomplish which two false positions were introduced. On the economic plane, a new criterion of "real planning" was presented to demonstrate the sociological dissimilarity of Czechoslovakia, Poland, Bulgaria, Rumania, Hungary as well as Yugoslavia from the USSR. Unfortunately, for this criterion, it not only, regardless of facts, forces the five satellite countries into the capitalist mold, but also Yugoslavia, and even calls into question our class definition of the USSR itself. On the social plane, the resolution arbitrarily deduced from the fact that because the present states came into being as a result not of victorious proletarian revolutions but of military-bureaucratic actions, *ipso facto* they cannot be sociologically similar to the USSR, except if the Kremlin annexes them into the USSR and integrates them into its own economy. This criterion is likewise false and dangerous because it forces its proponents to deny the reality of the overturn of property relations in the five satellite countries and draw hairsplitting distinctions between these and the property relations of the USSR; and in an attempt to maintain consistency with our program, forces them likewise into a whole series of theoretical innovations and contradictory formulations which necessarily reduce our Russian position to one of indescribable confusion and patchwork.

Let us examine these two main arguments of the IEC resolution in chronological order.

The resolution acknowledges that "the nationalization of industry, of the banking system, of communications and transport have been practically completed in Bulgaria, in Yugoslavia, and in Czechoslovakia; it is on the road to completion in Poland and in Hungary, and it has had a big start in Rumania. Wholesale trade is equally on the road to statification in most of these countries. Only retail trade and agriculture remain as yet largely in the hands of private proprietors." The further broad nationalization decrees promulgated in 1949 have swept into the statized sector practically all of banking, industry and transport in Poland, Hungary and Rumania as well, have made giant inroads into wholesale trade and have even bitten into retail trade. As a not untypical example, Rakosi announced in Parliament in August 1949 that 94 percent of wholesale trade and 25 percent of retail trade in Hungary was now transacted by the state.

But the resolution informs us that all these facts notwithstanding, "real planning" is impossible in these countries. Why? Because of the capitalist character of agriculture, and especially, as we have been lectured in our own discussion, the absence of nationalization of land; because of the narrow national frameworks, their lack of material resources and their dependence on the world market; and because of the mortgage the Kremlin has imposed on the economy of all these countries.

The resolution authors are starting the argumentation off on the wrong foot. They are guilty of confusing two different concepts—planning and socialist production. Planning can be effected when a state possesses the commanding heights of an economy and can determine, within the limits of its material possibilities, where to invest capital, on what lines to develop the economy, can eliminate to some degree the anarchy of the capitalist market and capitalist cyclical crises. Socialist production is another matter. For that you need a sufficiently high level of material resources, you have to be freed to a large degree from the pressure of the world market, you have to abolish the contradiction between agriculture and industry. That is why the arguments of the resolution, or any single one of them, are effective refutations of the possibility of organizing socialist production in one country, much less in such a small, poor country as Yugoslavia, or the impoverished and plundered East European satellite states. But they are not good arguments against the possibility of these countries, once their states have seized the commanding heights of the economy, of operating the economy in accordance with a plan, and to that extent, however inadequate it may be, eliminating the anarchy of capitalist production.

Comrade Germain is guilty of muddling up these two different concepts when he writes: "It does not at all follow . . . that *any* national framework whatever lends itself to planning on the mere condition that the proletariat had conquered power. . . . To *make a start* in the building of socialism in Rumania, in Luxembourg or in Paraguay is an even more patent absurdity than to pretend that this construction *is being completed* in the USSR." (*Fourth International,* September 1949) Not at all correct. One can argue about Luxembourg or Monte Carlo. But while the working class cannot build socialism in one country much less in small, undeveloped countries, precisely what it can do *is to make a start*, be it in Rumania or Paraguay, even though its efforts may not be as impressive as was the case in the USSR. This line of argumentation is wrong in theory and flies in the face of the reality of what is happening in Yugoslavia, and the five satellite states. If socialist production is our criterion, we would have to apply it to the USSR as well, where socialist production also remains the music of the future.

How seriously do the factors listed in the resolution affect nonetheless the ability of these countries to organize the economies in accordance with a plan?

The capitalist character of agricultural production in all these countries undoubtedly constitutes a most serious obstacle to planning. Not primarily because of the absence of nationalization of the land. Such a measure would not of itself alter the mode of agricultural production and was never listed as a task for the transitional period in the old socialist program. Engels, in his article *The Peasant Problem in France and Germany*, wrote what has been considered the classic position of Marxism on this question. He says, "When we are in possession of the powers of the state, we shall not even dream of forcibly expropriating the poorer peasants, the small holders (with or without compensation), as we shall have to do in relation to the large landowners. Our task as regards the small holders will first of all consist in transforming their individual production and individual ownership into cooperative production and cooperative ownership, not forcibly, but by way of example, and by offering social aid for this purpose."

The reasons for such a policy are obvious. Capitalism develops industry far more rapidly and thoroughly than it does agriculture. While industry is brought to the point of social production under capitalist private ownership, agricultural production is carried on to a large extent on small individual family farms. The workers state, therefore, in a position to expropriate industry and the banks at once and operate them as state enterprises, can only develop agriculture to large-scale mechanized production, operating on big state farms, only gradually and by convincing the bourgeois-minded farmers that the change is beneficial and in their interests.

It is true that one of the first decrees adopted by the young Soviet Republic nationalized the land. But desirable and important as such a step is, as it lays the legal groundwork for further moves to limit and curb capitalist tendencies and accumulations on the countryside, it does not at all follow that workers states everywhere, and at all times, will necessarily adopt such a measure in the first stages of the transition period. In old Russia, the peasantry itself demanded land nationalization because of the predominantly feudal character of land ownership. As early as 1905 the All-Russian Peasant Union called for the abolition of private property in land. In other cases, however, in the face of the hostility of the peasantry, especially in view of their fears of confiscation after the experience of Stalinist forced collectivizations, a young workers state may forego for a period such a move and concentrate on a number of supplementary measures to curb accumulations in land and the growth of big capitalists on the countryside, while using its state power to encourage collectivization as a step toward eventual socialist production in agriculture.

All the same, once the big landowners and big farmers are crushed as a class, once the big estates and farms are expropriated (with or without land nationalization), the petty-bourgeoisie of the countryside, while it remains a petty-bourgeoisie, is incapable of playing an independent role, either politically or economically. They may place innumerable obstacles in the way of planned economy and create enormous difficulties, but they do not have the ability to overturn the essential policy of the workers state and to pull the economy in a capitalist direction. Statized industry and banking replaces the old capitalist millionaire cliques as the hub around which the agricultural spokes revolve.

We are handed Lenin's well-known statement: "Small individual exploitation generates capitalism and the bourgeoisie in a permanent way, every day, every minute, with an elemental force and on a mass scale," and we are informed that is exactly what is happening in all these countries. Let us examine the whole reality, not just a part of it.

First on the USSR. Agricultural production in the USSR remains to this day petty-bourgeois, as the collectives are not statized but petty-bourgeois enterprises, which after meeting taxes and other state obligations sell their produce on the market. The Kremlin has been forced to make further concessions to the peasantry by legally granting collective farms use of the land in perpetuity, and the individual collective farm families use of private plots of land on which they are permitted to keep livestock, and the produce of which they can dispose of in any way they see fit. Two decades of experience have demonstrated that while this petty-bourgeois mode of production undoubtedly continues to constitute a big disorganizing factor in the Soviet economy and remains an easy starting point for new capitalist growth and developments, nevertheless, the workers state power has the ability to control, regulate and dominate the course of agricultural production, prevent the emergence of a new strong capitalist class and the sabotaging of its economic plans.

The five Kremlin Dependencies as well as Yugoslavia are attempting, in one form or another, to emulate and carry through a similar policy of collectivization of agriculture, of curbing capitalist accumulation on the countryside, and of controlling and regulating, as far as they can, agricultural production.

In all these countries, the large and what would be considered in this country medium-sized estates and farms have been confiscated and the broken-up parcels distributed to the landless peasantry or converted into model state farms. The old landowning and rich farming interests have been ruined and crushed. *In all these countries* the maximum size of farms is limited by law, 75 acres in Yugoslavia, 123 in Poland, Czechoslovakia, Rumania, 142 in Hungary, etc. In all these countries land cannot be bought or sold without permission from the state authorities, and no resale whatsoever of the land is permitted that was received from the state when the large estates were confiscated and broken up. Moreover, all six states are embarked on special campaigns to induce the peasantry to organize into large-scale cooperative farms. They are trying to set up a network of state-owned tractor and machine stations to service the farm cooperatives, in order to control agricultural production as well as to raise its levels, and to be in a position to integrate it as much as possible into their overall planning. To this end, extraordinary concessions are being made to the cooperatives in the way of lower taxes, smaller grain deliveries, and the granting of cheap credits and technical assistance, while progressively heavier taxes and deliveries to the state are demanded from the richer individual farm holders. Even outside the cooperatives, which are told what and how much to produce the state regulates all agricultural production to an extent, by means of the trading cooperatives which act as middlemen between the farmer and the government.

Of course, the reality is far less radiant than the resolutions and the paper plans indicate. The peasants are entering the cooperatives very slowly and with great reluctance. In Yugoslavia, where the regime apparently practices a softer policy toward the peasant and permits the well-to-do to enter the farm cooperatives, it was announced that at the end of 1949 approximately 14 percent of the arable land was in the cooperative sector and another 6 percent worked by state farms. In Bulgaria in July 1949, 12 percent of the arable land was tilled by cooperatives, although its Five-Year Plan calls for 60 percent of agricultural output being produced by cooperatives at the end of the plan in 1953. Hungary in May 1949 had a membership in the cooperatives of 60,000 who accounted for only a little over 1 percent of the country's arable land, although the Minister of Agriculture, I. Czala, stated that now that the enemies of the people had been kicked out of the cooperative movement the task was to increase the membership to 1,200,000 by the end of the year! In Poland, the cooperative movement has made scarcely any headway at all in the face of the panic and opposition of the peasantry, but 10 percent of the land is worked by the state farms. Czechoslovakia has been experiencing similar difficulties as Poland.

Moreover, the farm cooperatives in Eastern Europe are somewhat more capitalistic in their organization than the collectives in the Soviet Union, the main difference being that in the cooperatives, the working members, in addition to payment in kind for the amount and type of work performed, receive rent for their land in proportion to the amount contributed to the cooperative.

Beginning with 1948, especially after the cold war got going in earnest with the start of the Marshall Plan, and especially Tito's break with the Kremlin, the quisling regimes embarked on an energetic policy of bringing the "class war" into the villages, curbing the capitalist elements and aligning agriculture with their general state plans. The Tito regime, after the Cominform denunciation of its pro-kulak policy, also apparently executed a determined left turn in its agricultural policy. Immediately all the acute ailments besetting the regime in the USSR in the twenties, which Trotsky made so familiar to us in the earlier days of our movement, struck all these countries with tenfold force. Attempting to fight their way out of their economic cul-de-sacs by "building socialism in one country," they embarked on vastly ambitious plans of industrialization. Since they lacked the machinery, resources, productive capacities or trained personnel, they began taking it out of the hides of the workers. Piece work and speedup were introduced in the plants, hours of work lengthened, the authority of management made absolute. The desperate nature of the difficulties was highlighted recently when in Yugoslavia, where there exists, in contradistinction to the satellite states, some enthusiasm for the plan, the regime was forced to give up the "voluntary labor brigade" system and institute a new system of contract labor which freezes the worker to his job.

At the same time, the lack of consumer products and the high prices of those manufactured deprived the farmers of incentive to produce, led to speculation and black marketeering. The regimes thereupon decided to solve the crisis with the Stalinist mailed fist, by bringing the "class struggle" into the countryside, carrying through forced seizures, executing sales to the state for prices little better than confiscatory, arresting and imprisoning farmers who resisted or disobeyed, and forced entrance into cooperatives. This struggle against the peasantry was prosecuted in all the satellite countries and assumed a truly ferocious character during 1948–49 in Bulgaria, Hungary and Rumania. In Bulgaria in 1948 quota deliveries totalled approximately 11 billion levas, while free market purchases stood at 715 million levas.

Stalinist adventurism produced such panic in the peasantry and led to so much sabotage and individual resistance that the regimes felt compelled to back down here and there. The resolution passed by the plenum of the Communist Party of Bulgaria in June 1949 indicates pretty clearly the state of affairs. A few excerpts are worth quoting: "Our party has admitted serious weaknesses and mistakes in its policy toward the peasant farmers. . . . Under the system of quota purchases, in many cases the total produce of farmers has been taken away at controlled prices . . . the peasants have accordingly lost interest in increasing production and improving quality. . . . By setting up labor cooperative farms in almost the whole of the country, the best fields around the villages have been illegally confiscated and given to these labor cooperative farms, while farmers who are not members, have been given in exchange poor land in remote parts. . . . The peasants are either infuriated or fall under the influence of reaction. . . . Some peasants have been compelled to join labor cooperative farms, thus violating the principle of voluntary membership." The plenum adopted a number of concessions to the peasantry, declared that it "wholeheartedly condemns these abuses and obliges all party organizations to launch a merciless struggle . . . for the immediate removal of all irregularities" etc., etc.

This bureaucratic maneuvering and adventurism of the Stalinist quisling regimes brings out fully the monstrosity of the East European economies and the patent absurdity of any talk of building socialism in one country, and in such bled, ruined and backward little countries, at that. They point up the grisly character of Stalinist planning. But what stands out with equal force is that the regimes, in emulating Stalinist policy in the USSR from 1929–, are curbing big capitalist accumulations in agriculture, are preventing the uncontrolled playing out of the natural economic laws and the emergence of a powerful kulak class, are forcing the peasantry to go along with their economic designs, even though all this is accomplished, as it was in the USSR under Stalin, at the cost of tremendous disorganization and waste, and at the cost of provoking the burning hatred of the peasantry. The disorganized and scattered peasantry can balk, sabotage, force some concessions from the regimes. Petty-bourgeois agricultural production is undoubtedly a prime factor in sharply limiting any economic plan; but in the absence of strong leadership and support from the cities, the peasantry is helpless to reverse the present trend toward collectivization, or overturn the general trend toward state-planned-and-operated economy.

*Thus, it is entirely correct to point to petty-bourgeois production in agriculture as an important obstacle limiting planning and a possible starting point for capitalist restoration. It is entirely wrong, however, to point to it as preventing planning and demonstrating the capitalist character of the countries involved.*

This lengthy excursion into agriculture was necessary because this point constitutes, in our opinion, the most serious argument, on the economic side, of the supporters of the IEC resolution. It will be possible to deal with the other factors under the economic heading in a more cursory manner, as they all follow essentially the same scheme of argumentation.

It is called to our attention that these states are dependent on the capitalist world market to a far greater degree than was or is the USSR, that they are thus subject to its oscillations and to capitalist exploitation by the operation of the law of the equalization of the average rate of profit. All true. As a matter of fact, one could add that even when they trade with the USSR, this law remains operative, as the transactions are based on world prices, at least for the Kremlin's products in the exchange. All these arguments were used with devastating logic years ago by Trotsky against Stalin to demonstrate—the impossibility of building socialism in one country. But no one up to now has thought that they were arguments against the possibility of organizing an economy in a given anticapitalist country in accordance with a plan.

Comrade Germain in an article in the September 1949 *Fourth International* makes much of the fact that Czechoslovakia may have to curtail its production plans if it does not regain some lost markets, how production in Poland would be seriously affected if the world price of coal fell. We can recall how seriously the first Five-Year Plan in the USSR was affected when the world price of wheat cracked in the thirties. We see today how the plan in Yugoslavia is being hurt by the Kremlin's embargo and Tito's inability to sell enough to the capitalist world. These factors demonstrate very clearly that planned economy in one country, especially a small poor country encircled by capitalism, is bound to be deformed, distorted, pitiable; but they do not prove that planning cannot be initiated and practiced. It is possible that capitalism, through its control of the world market, may choke a country like Yugoslavia, or by one means or another overturn the present government, but then we will be confronted with a new Yugoslavia, and not the present one.

The same applies to the discussion of the narrow national frameworks and inadequate resources of all these states, and their consequent inability to organize and plan their economies on any broad division of labor and develop the productive forces to any satisfactory extent. Again the analysis is absolutely correct provided it is not employed to prove the wrong thing. The Kremlin's decision to prevent the formation of a Balkan-Danubian Federation is one of its historic crimes against the peoples of these countries and demonstrates—by itself—that the Kremlin has no progressive mission, that it can only exercise control by brute force, and that its very expansion carries within itself the seeds of its own destruction. But this does not prove that planning, however inadequate it may be, is impossible in Czechoslovakia or Poland any more than it is in Yugoslavia.

The question of Kremlin pillage, dismantling of plants, reparations and the joint-stock corporations fall in reality into the same category as the previous propositions and cannot be said to render impossible the organization of planning. The brunt of Kremlin pillage and reparations demands fell on the so-called "ex-enemy" countries, Rumania, Hungary and Bulgaria, and not on Czechoslovakia, Poland or Yugoslavia. Moreover, the policy of unrestrained robbery without thought of consequences or of future relations was likewise abandoned after 1947, when the Kremlin broke the remaining power of the bourgeoisie and perfected its own quisling regimes. (Yugoslavia, as everyone acknowledges, is in a special category and must be discussed separately.)

The Kremlin, at first, apparently had no clear idea of just what its relations would be with these states. Only after the "cold war" with the West became an established fact, and after a series of fumbles and empirical experimentations, did it resolve on converting these countries into its own dependencies, with a relationship symmetrical, not identical, to that of a colony and an imperialist state. In the recent period—especially after the Tito break—it has made an attempt to permit these countries to build up their economies. The reparations in Hungary and Rumania have been scaled down. Loans have been extended in a number of cases. So-called Germany property seized as booty has been returned to Bulgaria.

Of course, the robbery of these dependent states continues by overcharging them for their imports from the USSR and underpaying them for their exports to the USSR, by occupation charges, by preventing them from fusing their economies, and by deforming their production to suit the needs and demands of the Kremlin masters. The joint-stock corporations, which represent in reality a legal form for collecting unlimited reparations, still operate in two of the six countries, Rumania and Hungary. But even here proportions have to be guarded. In Hungary, for which figures are available, less than four percent of all industry is involved in the joint-stock corporations. This brigandage of the Kremlin oligarchy, taken in its entirety, certainly condemns these countries to poverty and continued economic backwardness and dislocation. But it cannot—leaving aside the arguments on the social plane which we will discuss presently—negate the anticapitalist, and by that reason, workers character of these economies, any more than imperialist exploitation of a colony necessarily negates the capitalist character of such a country's economy.

One adroit polemicist has suggested that our whole argumentation on the economic side is wide of the mark because the IEC resolution simply points out the various factors that are obstacles to the structural assimilation of these countries into the USSR and that must be overcome if assimilation is to take place. The proponent of this argument forgets that a premise must be proven as well as asserted. The IEC resolution authors start from the arbitrary premise that in the absence of socialist revolutions, these satellite countries can become workers states only by being absorbed into the structure and economy of the USSR. This flies in the face of what has taken place in the six countries under discussion of Eastern Europe. We maintain that if the state structures and the economies of these countries are similar to that of the USSR, then they are of the same class type. Any other conclusion calls into question, among other things, our characterization of the USSR.

After belaboring us for weeks with "real planning," the capitalist character of East Europe's agriculture, the dependence of these countries on world trade, their narrow national frameworks and so on, this line of argumentation was suddenly dropped like a hot potato. The reason being that in the interim, a number of supporters of the IEC resolution had concluded that Yugoslavia was a workers state, and obviously these economic criteria—if correct—were as valid for Yugoslavia as for Poland or Czechoslovakia. Since that time the discussion has shifted in the main to the arguments on the social plane, the questions of the state structure of these countries, the implications of the positions with regard to Marxist theory and the nature of Stalinism; and that is the main burden of Comrade Germain's most recent discussion article on the question as well.

Let us begin our consideration of this aspect of the question by reviewing briefly the 1944–45 events.

The Red Army's entrance into Eastern Europe everywhere gave an impulse to the socialist revolution. There was a big uprising in Prague in May 1945. Czechoslovakia was soon dotted by a network of Committees, which were organs of power, even though of a bowdlerized variety. (Unlike soviets, their members were selected from all the National Front parties, including the bourgeois parties. They were, however, dominated by the representatives of the working class parties, the Stalinists and Social Democrats.) Workers Councils sprang up in the plants and in the first period exercised control over production. The *London Economist* correspondent reported: "When the country was liberated, the councils and committees were really more powerful than the central government, which had no armed forces at its disposal and which came in from abroad at the heels of the victorious Russians." It must be recalled that the Partisan movement attained great proportions in Czechoslovakia, being second only to Yugoslavia and Greece. The movement was strong enough that a Slovak National Council could be set up by 1943 which led an uprising in Slovakia in August 1944 and proclaimed on September 1 of that year its assumption of power and the establishment of the Czechoslovak Republic (which the Nazis shortly defeated).

A big uprising likewise took place in September 1944 in Sofia which swept the existing government out of power. So-called Fatherland Front Committees, similar to the committees in Czechoslovakia, sprang up throughout Bulgaria, wielded power on a local scale, and in many cases attempted a revolutionary settlement with the native fascist tyrants. The correspondents reported that in the capitol red flags were flying over the government buildings as over thousands of homes, of the arrest of great numbers of fascists by the armed masses, of huge demonstrations, of a railway strike that paralyzed all activity.

Ferenc Nagy, former Premier of Hungary, describes the situation in that country during this period in his book, *The Struggle Behind the Iron Curtain:* "The disintegration of the government of the country opened the way for Communist penetration. None of the old town councils or municipal assemblies remained; the new political order substituted for them transitory administrative bodies called 'national committees,' with unlimited power. Assuming control of the municipalities, townships, and even cities, they appointed their own men as elders, councilors, and committeemen to pass judgment upon the political past and present of each citizen. The national committees managed the scant food supply; few aspects of daily life escaped their control. This situation was not peculiar to Hungary."

Exactly right. It was duplicated in Rumania on almost identical lines, and even in Poland, where the masses were very suspicious of and largely hostile to the new regime and the Red Army because of Stalin's betrayal of the 1944 Warsaw uprising and his terror against left-wing elements in Eastern Poland.

As for Yugoslavia, we are all acquainted that a civil war raged from 1941 on, that Committees were set up as new organs of power in the territories taken by the Partisans, and that similar Committees were appointed and began functioning in the major centers after Tito's forces marched in with the Red Army into Belgrade.

In all these countries the pre-war regimes and pre-war state structures had collapsed and had been replaced with new ones. Comrade Germain in his recent article admits that the old state apparatus was smashed in the course of the war in at least Czechoslovakia, Poland and Yugoslavia. To these three countries we will add at least two more, Hungary and Bulgaria.

In Hungary, the native fascists had been infiltrating the state apparatus throughout the war period until they won complete control in the Szalasi coup d'etat in 1944. With the retreat of the Nazi forces at the end of that year, the Szalasi government, including every official of any consequence, likewise moved westward, and for a brief time it even persisted as a government-in-exile. Whatever officials of the old regime remained behind were not ruling anything or anybody, but skulking in the cellars. Ferenc Nagy, in the book previously referred to, states: "Local administration had fallen into chaos. Most officials had fled to the west, particularly if they had dealt with the Nazis. A large proportion of the reliable civil employees had been transferred forcibly to Germany.... The old police, branded as the tool of the former reactionary government, was disbanded, and a new force hurriedly organized." The Stalinists have the same estimation. Zoltan Deak, editor of *Magyar Jovo,* describes in *Hungary's Fight for Democracy* the period at the end of 1944: "There was no administrative force left in the country, almost all of them had fled with the Nazis."

The picture was no different in Bulgaria. Again both the Stalinists and the capitalist reactionaries agree on the facts. Ilya Ehrenburg, in his work *European Crossroad,* declares: "What happened in September 9, 1944 was not a mere change of ministries, but a change of government. The whole governmental apparatus of the fascists was destroyed.... In Bulgaria 11,000 fascists, including diplomats, courtiers, glamour girls, and profiteers, were handed over to the tribunals as war criminals." R.H. Markham, the reactionary correspondent of the *Christian Science Monitor,* writes in his book on Tito that as the Red Army advanced into Bulgaria, "all authority broke down and every Bulgarian became his own master. At that moment a group of conspirators, organized in the Fatherland

Front and led by Communists, reached out their hands and took the reins of power, which they still hold. . . . The courts were set up by self-appointed Fatherland Front Committees. They did not emanate from nor were they controlled by the Ministry of Justice, the Cabinet, or the Supreme Court." Dragoicheva, in an official report, describes the activities of the Fatherland Front during the first six months of its existence. It formed 7,292 Committees throughout the country, which "controlled" the government, and in many cases "functioned as the government." About 59 percent of the members of the Committees were "Communists," 36 percent Agrarians, 3 percent Social Democrats, 2 percent Zvenoists.

The one country in which the old state structure was able to partially maintain itself, for a while, anyhow, was Rumania, because of the fast footwork of the old ruling classes and the treachery of the Kremlin agents. And even here, as the facts show, it was of brief duration.

Comrade Germain insists, however, that even in Czechoslovakia and Poland, where the old structures were wiped out, new bourgeois states under Stalinist domination were set up, using whatever old bricks were still lying around for the reconstruction job. We thus arrive at the triumphant "Marxist" conclusion that "bourgeois states" have been engaged for *four years* in expropriating the landed estates and large farms and distributing them to the landless peasantry, in destroying the old landlord and agricultural bourgeois classes, in curbing in the most violent and brutal fashion capitalist developments in the countryside and pushing a collectivization policy designed to control and harness agricultural production; for *four years,* supposedly "bourgeois states" have been expropriating, in the main, the urban capitalists and statizing all the essential parts of the economy, banking, industry, transport, wholesale trade and even some retail trade, and organizing the economy in accordance with a plan; and finally, these same "bourgeois states" have been systematically and violently purging and wiping out the remains of the political power of the bourgeoisie, destroying its points of support in the state apparatus and replacing it with an administrative apparatus which in all essentials resembles the one in the USSR. Some bourgeois states! And this phantasmagoria is handed us—with solemn mien—in the name of theoretical orthodoxy and Marxist methodology. We now have to add to our previous categories a new one of bourgeois states of such unique variety that rather than being the guardians of bourgeois property relations, are its executioners.

The comrades apparently have an uneasy feeling that everything is not in order here, so they try to divert our attention with irrelevancies. We are informed that there remain a lot of ex-fascists, capitalists and former functionaries in the present state apparatus. We can be sure there are. But that has no decisive significance. The important question is: Who determines policy? Who runs who? Are the bourgeois opportunists serving under the orders and policy of the Stalinists, or are the Stalinists serving under the orders and policy of the bourgeois elements? Everyone knows the answer. Let us recall in this connection that Trotsky wrote in 1936—fourteen years ago—that a bourgeois counterrevolution in the USSR would have to clean out far fewer of the personnel in the state apparatus than a proletarian political revolution. No one in our ranks has heretofore deduced from this that the state in the USSR was bourgeois in character.

Germain, in another attempt to extricate himself out of this difficulty, informs us of the existence in history of Bonapartist regimes that are in conflict with their economies. Yes, Trotsky taught us this long ago. But such a conflict signifies a condition of civil war, which will be brought to a conclusion either by the state reconstructing the economy in its own class image, or the class forces of the economy overthrowing the state and setting up a new one in harmony with their economy. How is this an explanation for the analysis in Eastern Europe where for four years supposedly "bourgeois states" have not been bringing the economy into harmony with their own class nature but constantly widening the contradiction between the two? Some Bonapartist regimes may lift themselves above the classes and represent the interests of the dominant class only in the last analysis. That does not permit us to stretch the formula another notch and suggest that they need not represent these class interests at all. That would be a denial of the class theory of the state.

A study of the actual happenings in these countries provides the key for an exit out of this theoretical blind alley. The states set up in all these countries in 1945—including Yugoslavia—were not simply bourgeois but regimes of dual power. The power of the working class was soon overwhelmed as an independent force by the Stalinist bureaucracy which harnessed it in its own interests, resided in the local and district committees, the workers militias, the newly created Stalinist-controlled police force and judiciary, buttressed, of course, by the all-powerful Red Army occupation forces. The bourgeoisie still retained a measure of power through its ownership of great sectors of the economy, its political organizations, press, and elements of governmental power. This dual power assumed the unique form of central coalition governments which formally were pledged not to alter the pre-war social character of these countries. Because the Stalinists, under the Kremlin dictate, wanted the alliance with the bourgeoisie to help fasten their bureaucratic grip on the working masses, and because they still had no clear perspectives of their future course. And on the other side, the debilitated bourgeoisie grasped at these alliances as the only means by which they could even hope to reconstitute their rule.

*Only in this sense, only within the strict limitations of the dual power character of these regimes, was it permissible to still call these new states capitalist in the 1945 period.* The relationship of strength in the dual power varied from country to country, from Czechoslovakia, as the extreme on one end, to Yugoslavia on the other. In the former, the bourgeoisie retained a lot of class strength and was a real factor in the coalition. In Yugoslavia its power had been decisively broken during the protracted civil war, and it was little more than a captive in the coalition. But in every case the Stalinists were the dominant force. This was demonstrated conclusively later on by the ease with which they broke the back of the bourgeoisie politically and economically, and finally eliminated the dual power in favor of their exclusive power.

All of us are aware that the Kremlin did not give free rein to the workers to carry their revolutions through to the end, but on the contrary, suppressed the independent actions of the masses, put its heavy hand on their organizations, and sidetracked the movement into the channels of the coalition governments. Their role was politically counterrevolutionary. But the Kremlin did not wipe out these new organs of power as would a bourgeois counterrevolution. They bureaucratized them. They took over control and reshaped them as instruments of their own purposes, and finally as the new administrative structure of their sovereignty. The swift strangulation of the workers' independent movement and the victory of the bureaucracy was due, as in 1939, to the workers' isolation from the international labor movement and their insufficient organization in the face of the Kremlin's overpowering strength.

The facts are plain that in every case confiscation of the estates and the distribution of the land was carried through by a great network of local committees, which then remained as administrative organs for the Stalinist regimes on the countryside. The Workers Councils in Czechoslovakia, to take another example, were not abolished, but transformed into part of the "new aristocracy" by electing their representatives from single lists, providing that these representatives no longer be required to do manual work, and to be paid for all extra time spent on special duties. The committees, which took over the functions of the former municipal bodies, were incorporated into the state apparatus by special decrees. Even the "action committees" organized by the Stalinists in 1948 to bring the capitalists to heel, have not been disbanded but, we read, "are to become permanent institutions to safeguard the victory won during the crisis." The police, the army, the judiciary have been thoroughly overhauled, reorganized and placed under new leadership.

The next stage came after the sharpening of the cold war and the Kremlin's determination to consolidate its hold on these dependencies. The Stalinist bureaucratic cliques, using their crushing superiority, and resting on the new administrative organs under their command, proceeded, step by step, to exterminate the bourgeois parties and drive their representatives out of the governments and committees, with the most prominent sent to the gallows, or prisons, or forced into exile. They then forced through the purge of the Social Democratic parties and their prison unification with the Stalinists. In the same period, new decrees were promulgated which, in effect, expropriated the remaining sections of the bourgeoisie, and placed all the levers of economic power in the hands of the now totalitarianized regimes.

*With the elimination of the remains of bourgeois power, the new police governments issued new constitutions during 1948–49, all modeled on the 1936 Stalinist constitution and based on the new administrative organs of the state. These constitutions were the juridical expression of the fact that the dual power regimes had come to an end, that the de facto civil war had been resolved in favor of the Stalinist power, and that the new states could therefore no longer be regarded as capitalist even in the limited form that we have previously employed it, but were now guardians of the new property relations based on expropriated and nationalized property, and hence of the same class character as the USSR.*

This whole development revealed again, as it did in 1939 in Eastern Poland, the dual role of the Kremlin oligarchy. On the one hand, it cannot tolerate a free working class movement and must suppress it to preserve itself. In ordinary circumstances, this need to exercise dictatorial control over the labor movement and its policy of maneuvering between the proletariat and bourgeoisie, inevitably disarms the workers' movement and reinforces the capitalist power, as it did in France and Italy in this same period. On the other hand, this caste cannot share power with the capitalists because it rests on the sociological remains of the Russian Revolution. Hence, in the special circumstances prevailing in these adjoining countries in the years after the war, where the Kremlin's might was so overwhelming it could impose its own will on the proletariat with the aid of the bourgeoisie and then in turn, resting on its new bureaucratized apparatus, crush this enfeebled bourgeoisie. This is what occurred in Eastern Europe. To deny it is to deny reality.

What is the answer of the comrades on the other side to these facts? They have shifted the discussion to the doctrinal plane. Let us see how matters stand here.

We are accused of economism because it is claimed we have created a simple equation that nationalized economy equals a workers state. But have we not witnessed extensive nationalizations in England, France, Norway, and Comrade Germain, in his researches, has even dug up a paper decree for nationalization issued by Mussolini in Northern Italy, and tossed it into the discussion for whatever it is worth. These analogies are all arbitrary and false. We certainly ought to be able to distinguish between capitalist and anticapitalist nationalizations. The nationalizations in Western Europe were all carried through with the approval, or at least the acquiescence, of the capitalist class. The capitalists, after the nationalizations, became state rentiers, and often remained the managers of the concerns involved. And all this was done under the aegis of a capitalist state maintained intact, capitalist property relations maintained intact, and a capitalist class whose dominant position continued undisturbed. There could be reasonable question in 1945 as to the precise character of the first nationalizations in Czechoslovakia, Poland and Yugoslavia, as they were executed under ambiguous formulas, and the class character of the states involved was still not settled. There can be no doubt concerning their class character today.

Beneath all the deceptive and sly Stalinist legal formulas governing the nationalizations stands out the dominant fact that, in the main, the properties of the native capitalist classes have been expropriated, and that these classes have been politically crushed. Numbers of individual capitalists have undoubtedly been able to save themselves by going to work for the new rulers, by stealing, by blackmarketeering and bribe-taking. But the class has been expropriated and ruined. The press of these countries bristles with news accounts which testify to the accuracy of this evaluation. The first series of nationalizations which expropriated "German," "enemy," and "collaborationist" properties broke the back of the weak bourgeoisies and placed the lion's portion of urban economy in the state sector, 82 percent of industry in Yugoslavia, almost 2/3 in Czechoslovakia, 40 percent in Poland; as well as most banking operations. In the later nationalization decrees, which took over the properties of the native capitalists, state nationalization funds were set up in a number of countries to ostensibly compensate the former owners. Even where payments were actually made, the transactions were little short of confiscatory, while on the whole, compensation was honored more in the breach than the observance.

The sweeping and anticapitalist character of the 1945–46 nationalizations in Yugoslavia is too well known to require elaboration. But, even in the case of the Tito government, which emerged, unlike any of the others, out of the civil war, these were carried through by means of deceptive slogans and ambiguous methods. Kidric, in his economic report to the Fifth Congress of the Yugoslav Communist Party, explains: "The principal form of this offensive (against the capitalist positions in the economy) were the court procedures against traitorous reactionaries which regularly ended, aside from other things, with the confiscation of their properties." In addition, monetary manipulation, two-price systems, state control over raw materials, and progressive taxation were deliberately employed in every case to ruin the bourgeoisie, and as instruments of expropriation. Thus, while the 1947 nationalization decree in Bulgaria officially indemnified former proprietors with interest-bearing bonds redeemable in 20 years; the 1948 nationalization law in Rumania provided for compensation by state bonds redeemable against profits realized in the former owner's plants; and the 1948 nationalization decrees in Yugoslavia and the 1949 decrees in Hungary called for compensation of former owners with state bonds, the chief interest of all these decrees and laws is for a study of Stalinist methods rather than in any importance they possessed in maintaining the native capitalist classes.

Here are a few samples of how they operated in practice: Immediately after the publication of the Rumanian nationalization law, it was announced that no compensation would be paid to persons who enriched themselves illegally, or who left Rumania illegally, or who would not agree to return; while the press was filled with reports of arrests of former owners for economic sabotage. On October 5, 1948, the Presidium of the Grand National Assembly deprived a number of persons of their citizenship, including N. and C. Malaxa and Max Ausnit, Rumania's biggest industrialists, with all their property confiscated by the state. The *London Economist* explained in detail that the pretense of compensation in the Bulgarian nationalization laws was fraudulent: "In reality this nationalization was the naked confiscation of all property and spelt the liquidation of the middle classes." The same *de facto* confiscation occurred in Czechoslovakia, where in July 1949 a bill was passed giving the Minister of the Interior the right to deprive all those of citizenship who lived abroad, or engaged in activities hostile to the state, or who had gone abroad illegally, or failed to return within 30 to 90 days if summoned by the Minister of the Interior.

It is true that in a number of cases foreign Allied capitalists received compensation for their properties, this being the price that the East-European countries had to pay for loans or trade credits from the West, or to get back their gold supplies from England or the United States. But this cannot be given any decisive weight in Yugoslavia any more than in Poland or Hungary. To say, therefore, as Comrade Germain does (*Fourth International,* May 1949) that in none of these countries has the bourgeoisie been reduced "to a point comparable in Russia during the period of the NEP" is to contradict the facts.

So much for the anticapitalist character of these nationalizations. There is another important aspect to this question. It is putting the thing on its head to claim that we say nationalizations equal a workers state. The correct way to put the matter is that only an anticapitalist, therefore a workers, state can nationalize the whole economy and operate it in accordance with a plan. We have heretofore denied the capacity of capitalism to do it. Trotsky, writing 58 years after Engels' *Anti-Dühring,* and basing himself on the greater experiences of the development of capitalism, wrote: "Under an integral 'State Capitalism,' this law of the equal rate of profit would be realized, not by devious routes—that is, competition among different capitals—but immediately and directly through state bookkeeping. Such a regime never existed, however, and, because of profound contradictions among the proprietors themselves, never will exist—the more so since, in its quality of universal repository of capitalist property, the state would be too tempting an object for social revolution." (*Revolution Betrayed*, New York, Pathfinder, 1937, 1972, p. 255 [2013 printing].)

The British labor government has gone further in nationalizing sectors of the economy than probably any of us envisaged in the past. Can we therefore conclude that this process can go on indefinitely until all commanding heights of the economy are in the hands of the state? Not according to our theory. As a matter of fact, the capitalist opposition to the steel nationalization gave forewarning that at a certain point the bourgeoisie would resist with every weapon at its command. And if, under the impulsion of pressure from the masses, the Labour Party would nevertheless—in the teeth of capitalist hostility—proceed with its nationalization program, that would lead to a decisive clash and the beginning of civil war in the British Isles. And for precisely the reason given by Trotsky: "In its quality of universal repository of capitalist property, the state would be too tempting an object for social revolution."

In their anxiety to find formal analogies to refute our position, the comrades are opening the door wide to Comrade Johnson's theories of state capitalism, and endowing capitalism with the possibility of entering a new higher stage, under which the economy would be statized and operated in a planned manner. The suggestion that a capitalist state can nationalize "the greatest part of the means of production and exchange" is an innovation in our ideology. We are not unjustified in demanding that this be proven, and its consequences for our program explained to us, and not just tossed out in the course of the discussion—in passing.

We are informed that Marxism-Leninism holds that the transition from a capitalist to a workers state can only be effected by "the violent destruction of the bourgeois state apparatus and the establishment of a new type of state apparatus" and that therefore we are compelled, on the basis of our analysis, to revise the Marxist-Leninist theory of the state. Before we have any glib talk of revising Marxism, let us check back on what the classics have to say on this score.

Marx's discussion of this question is contained in his well-known April 12, 1871 letter to Kugelman, where he states: "If you look at the last chapter of my *Eighteenth Brumaire,* you will see that I declare the next attempt of the French Revolution to be: not merely to hand over, from one set of hands to another, the bureaucratic and military machine—as has occurred hitherto—but to *shatter* it; and it is this that is the preliminary condition of any real people's revolution on the Continent." Lenin in *State and Revolution* explains that Marx confined his conclusions to the Continent because he "excluded England, where a revolution, even a people's revolution, could be imagined, and was then possible *without* the preliminary condition of the destruction 'of the available machinery of the state'."

In his address in 1872 to the Hague Convention of the International, Marx further stated: "The worker must one day capture political power in order to found the new organization of labor. He must reverse the old policy, which the old institutions maintain, if he will not, like the Christians of old who despised and neglected such things, renounce the things of this world. But we do not assert that the way to reach this goal is the same everywhere. We know that the institutions, the manners, and the customs of the various countries must be considered, and we do not deny that there are countries like England and America, and if I understood your arrangements better, I might even add Holland, where the worker may attain his object by peaceful means. But not in all countries is this the case."

To complete the quotations, it is necessary to add that Lenin in his *State and Revolution* concluded that, "Today in 1917, in the epoch of the first great imperialist war, this distinction of Marx's becomes unreal."

These quotations from the classics are not being adduced to suggest at this late date the possibility of a peaceful transition today in England, America, or Eastern Europe. They are introduced to show the *development* of Marxist thought on this question based on living experiences. Naturally, Marx, and Lenin in 1917, knew nothing of Stalinist degeneration, and concluded that the working class could get itself into a position where it could shatter the old state machinery only by winning political power by means of a mass uprising. But in the meantime a new phenomenon has come into the picture: A workers state which is today ruled by a reactionary oligarchy, and which was able to enter Eastern Europe at the end of the war, and under the special circumstances and in the specific territories, control the working class movement, and utilize this control to shatter the old bourgeois states and erect new ones in their place. Wherein is there any revision of Marxism here any more than in Trotsky's explanation of the change-over in Eastern Poland in 1939?

The remaining arguments on the doctrinal front reduce themselves to the flat assertion that the capitalist state can be shattered and a new state created only by means of a classic socialist revolution, or the absorption of territories into the USSR; and since neither one nor the other has taken place in Eastern Europe, they cannot be workers states, regardless of the facts. It is of course difficult, if not impossible, to deal with this type of argument. The question is: is it any good?

Why couldn't it happen, regardless of what the facts show? We are advised that it is absurd to imagine that tens of thousands of vital economic relations can be destroyed and new ones substituted in their place without the action of the masses, and that the Kremlin could only accomplish this in the territories it incorporated into the USSR by physically exterminating or deporting all capitalists, big and medium peasants, the middle classes, etc.

Here are the facts. The deportations in the Baltics and Eastern Poland were of the same order as the deportations from the Ukraine after the war; they were motivated, in the first instance, by the political needs of the Kremlin and not designed to effect any social overturns. The big deportations in the Baltics took place in 1940; the collectivization of agriculture occurred only in 1948. The descriptions of the deportations show the Kremlin authorities were trying to wipe out all potential sources of opposition, and not putting through any social or economic program. The Kremlin made no appeal whatsoever to the Baltic masses, even of a limited variety. It was interested solely in clearing "politically unreliable" elements out of this strategic area, and very likely, solving manpower shortages in its slave labor camps, at the same time. The 200,000 deported out of a population of 6 million in the three Baltic countries were invariably picked on the basis of "political unreliability," whether it was "Trotskyism" or "correspondence with abroad," and not class position.

Moreover, we see in the recent dispatches that the Czech Stalinists are deporting recalcitrant capitalists, or just ordinary political opponents, to the uranium mines at Jachymov, or the coal mines at Kladno. All the other satellites, we can be sure, have not been behind in setting up their own slave labor or concentration camps in strict accordance with the latest methods of the Kremlin sadists. It is safe to assume, we believe, that 99 times out of 100 a trip to Jachymov is just as effective as a trip to Siberia.

Our versatile opponents, as if aware that their foregoing argument may have proven not sufficiently impressive, present us with one—that is its direct opposite. Trotsky said in 1939 in discussing Eastern Europe, we are told, that without an appeal to independent activity on the part of the masses it was impossible to constitute a new regime, even though on the morrow the masses would be suppressed by ruthless police measures. The Kremlin made such an appeal in 1939 in Eastern Poland, but in 1945, instead, the Stalinists first concluded agreements with the bourgeoisie to regiment the masses. How could the bureaucracy accomplish, without mobilizing the masses, that which Trotsky said could only be accomplished by such a mobilization?

This objection is really laughable. In 1939 the Kremlin came into Eastern Poland by means of an agreement with Hitler, which was the signal for the Second World War. The international working class movement was at its lowest point. The native population was suspicious of the invading Red Army troops. The situation was absolutely cold. In order to win a modicum of support from the masses to constitute the new regimes and wipe out bourgeois influence, the Kremlin had to make some limited appeals to the workers and peasants. In 1945 the Kremlin entered an Eastern Europe aflame with revolution. It wasn't a pact with Hitler that brought them in, but the smashup of the Nazi machine by the triumphant Red Army. These victories gave an impetus to the revolution, and not only in Eastern Europe. The workers, and to a degree the peasants, were on the move. The problem, from the Kremlin's viewpoint, was not how to encourage the masses, but how to suppress their initiative and domesticate their organizations. To be able to see the limited independent activity of the masses in 1939 in Eastern Poland, and not to be able to see the ten-times greater and profounder activity of the masses in Eastern Europe in 1945, is truly a case of steeling oneself against the reality in order to maintain a preconceived thesis.

Trotsky considered that the events in Eastern Poland in 1939 added up to a civil war. "Naturally, this is a civil war of a special type," he wrote. "It does not arise spontaneously from the depths of the popular masses. It is not conducted under the leadership of the Finnish revolutionary party based on mass support. It is introduced on bayonets from without. It is controlled by the Moscow bureaucracy." (*In Defense of Marxism*, p. 172.)

If we accept Trotsky's method of reasoning, how can we characterize the events in Eastern Europe from 1945 to 1949—the expropriation of the bourgeoisie, the crushing of its political power, the setting up of new state structures, the planned organization of the economy—except as a civil war of a special variety that ended with the destruction of the capitalist states and the institution of new anticapitalist states.

"None of these quotations from Trotsky's 1939 writings apply," we are sternly warned. Trotsky was talking only of territories to be incorporated into the USSR, and these dependent countries have not been incorporated. This is an incomprehensible argument. Trotsky was discussing territories which the Kremlin planned to incorporate into the USSR. But he nowhere said that this development could not take place except on the basis of incorporation into the USSR. Naturally, it is not a question of finding out precisely what took place in Eastern Europe in 1945–49 by reading Trotsky's analysis of 1939. But his method of reasoning applies with full force to the post-war happenings. If the Kremlin in 1939 was able to effect a change in property relations while subjecting the masses to its own bureaucratic control in Eastern Poland—because of the prostration of the bourgeoisie, and the insufficient organization of the masses—why was an essentially similar process impossible when similar relationships obtained in Western Poland or Czechoslovakia, irrespective of whether these territories eventually will or will not be incorporated into the USSR? This is to invest borders with mystic significance.

But, it is further objected, the East Polish economy was integrated into that of the USSR, while the economies of the satellite countries have not been. That is true, but not decisive. The property relations of these countries are similar to that of the USSR, and that is what is decisive in considering their sociological character.

To conclude this section: Only on the basis of our evaluation are the developments accounted for in strict accordance both with the facts and with the Marxist method, without having to introduce new criteria of "real planning," without opening the door to a theory of state capitalism, without undermining our position on the USSR and the consistency of our world program, and without the necessity for new tortured formulas of combined developments, where one and the same regime promulgates both bourgeois and proletarian nationalizations, and of Bonapartist regimes without any definite class base.

Now, we come to the important question of what conclusions flow from this analysis. In the SWP discussion, the argument has been pressed with great vigor that our analysis, willy-nilly, leads to the theory of the bureaucratic revolution; that if Stalinism can overturn capitalism and build the new society by its police-bureaucratic methods, what role remains for the Fourth International? We could criticize their excesses and undemocratic methods, but that is an insufficient foundation for the maintenance and building of a new international organization. So runs the argument. Despite its heavy pretense of "thinking things through," this is just a hollow debater's point. First, the reality in Eastern Europe must be recognized regardless of where it leads. But we do not maintain that the Kremlin every place and everywhere can carry through the overturns that it was able to accomplish under the unique conditions that existed at the end of the war in these adjacent countries. We do not maintain that these overturns can furnish the pattern for the road to power, any more than did the overturn in Eastern Poland in 1939.

If, however, despite our precise limitation of the East European events, we simply must—so we are told—give these overturns a universal application, why is the other side relieved of this same necessity? Here are comrades who have adopted a resolution which talks of "the disappearing bourgeoisie of the buffer zone," "bourgeoisie is not the dominant class," "the statization of economy," etc., etc. All right. These are not workers states. Let us say these are neocapitalist states, state capitalist states, or what have you. Why doesn't this have—

using your logic—universal application? If Stalinism could create these types of new capitalist states in Eastern Europe, doesn't that mean it can do the same thing in Western Europe, Asia, and the South Sea Islands? Does pinning a capitalist label on these states relieve you of the necessity of considering the developments in Eastern Europe as unique?

How are the comrades who vote together with the supporters of the IEC resolution, but maintain, nevertheless, that Yugoslavia is a workers state, how are they in a superior position? You comrades have declared that ex-Stalinist centrists, the Titoists, have carried through a successful workers revolution, have destroyed the bourgeois state and created a workers state. Doesn't that—if everything must be given universal application—invest Titoism with a historic future? Doesn't that imply—employing your logic—that instead of trying to teach the Titoists, we ought to enroll in their school on how to make successful revolutions and build workers states? This is a knife that cuts both ways.

Stalinist expansion is a fact, not a theory. It stems not from this or that characterization of the East European states but from the Kremlin's emergence from the war as the second world power, and the weakening of the bourgeoisie. This expansion, however, cannot just go on indefinitely. It has sharply defined limits. For two reasons: First, the Kremlin's savagely nationalistic policy has already led to the Tito break, may well produce similar breaks in the Far East on the morrow, and has produced indescribable tensions and crises in all of the satellites. In the new context, the Kremlin's conduct towards these states reveals anew that this oligarchy has no historic future, that it cannot be the instrument for the destruction of world capitalism and the institution of a new society. Second, the Kremlin's troops cannot move beyond their present spheres of influence without that becoming the signal for the next war; and the Kremlin will not be the initiator of the war. That is why we can discuss the possibility of the Red Army overrunning parts of Europe and Asia only in the context of the Third World War. It may be that under such circumstances the Kremlin would attempt to follow a policy roughly similar to its *initial* policy in Eastern Europe in 1945. But all this, as well as how much territory each side occupies, would be simply incidents in the war. The future of humanity would be decided by more important considerations: The outcome of the war, and the progress of socialist revolutions.

Comrade Germain believes that our analysis implies the possibility of the military victory of Stalinism in a new world war. It is difficult to follow the logic. What do our official documents say on this? "A third world war, in the form of an attack of world imperialism—under American leadership—against the USSR is inevitable if successful socialist revolutions do not materialize in the interim. If the contest between the USSR and world imperialism is confined, however, to military means, the defeat and destruction of the USSR is certain." The reason? Obviously, because world imperialism is far stronger than the USSR, materially, technically, culturally. How does our characterization of the East European happenings overturn this estimation?

But we have every reason to believe that in the event that humanity is thrust into a new slaughter, it will not be imperialism that will be the victor. After the partisan movements that swept Europe in the course of the last war, the uprisings in Italy and Greece, the rise of Tito to power in Yugoslavia, and the revolutionary aftermath in the Far East, we have every reason to believe that this time the socialist storm will be fiercer, and will start earlier. And after the Tito development, we have every reason to believe that it will assert its independence of and opposition to the Kremlin traitors. The socialist revolution will not only paralyze the hands of imperialism, but will inaugurate the process which will disintegrate the parasitic structure of Stalinism. Our basic perspective remains unchanged.

One final word: We are living in a world of rapidly changing events and many unexpected developments. Our cadres, which still have the job everywhere of fusing themselves with the mass movement, must be able to tenaciously stick to their principles, and at the same time have the capacity to orient themselves in every new difficult situation, and adjust themselves to the necessary tactical requirements. Our militants must feel that it is possible to carry through discussion in our movement in a calm atmosphere, free of bigotry. Any call in the present discussion for the stalwarts to rally round the flag is gratuitous, because the flag is not being assailed. The discussion should be carried through, without factionalism, until all the arguments are in, and the membership, in its collective wisdom, can render its decision.

Report to the Congress

# EVOLUTION OF EASTERN EUROPE

By Pierre Frank

The Soviet buffer zone of Eastern Europe, which came into being after the Second World War, has aroused lively discussions in and around our ranks. Our opinions have evolved and we have rectified errors committed on this question in the past years. Today the evolution of the buffer zone countries on a number of fundamentals has been completed in an irreversible manner. Our ideas have been clarified on several important questions such as the nature of these states and the conclusions to be derived therefrom. The resolution submitted to the Congress registers our progress in this matter. It is not without value to view this problem from as broad a viewpoint as possible, to first of all retrace the road we have traveled.

## The history of the buffer zone question

At the end of the Second World War, as a result of the Potsdam agreements, the entire world was confronted with a zone of influence of the Soviet Union in Eastern Europe. The Russian state—which we considered a degenerated workers' state—dominated a series of capitalist states militarily and politically; coalition governments between Stalinists and bourgeois politicians were constituted; the capitalist economies were not fundamentally uprooted, although important changes had been introduced.

Molotov had declared at the first occasion, in the name of the Soviet government, when Russian troops entered Rumanian territory, that his government had no intention of altering the social system of these countries. The only and avowed desire of the Kremlin in these countries was to replace the hostile governments of the past (the *cordon sanitaire* at the end of the First World War) by governments friendly to the USSR. But we understood at that time that what was involved was not the desires of the Kremlin bureaucracy. The workers' state, and not only the bureaucracy, would have its influence on the new territories. What could this lead to?

On the theoretical plane we took as our point of departure our definition of the USSR and Trotsky's succinct remarks in *In Defense of Marxism* on the question of territories occupied by the USSR and susceptible to integration within it. These remarks have been cited many times in our discussions and are certainly known to all the comrades present here. Let us only refer to this one:

> Let us for a moment conceive that in accordance with the treaty with Hitler, the Moscow government leaves untouched the rights of private property in the occupied areas and limits itself to 'control' after the fascist pattern. Such a concession would have a deep-going principled character and might become the starting point for a new chapter in the history of the Soviet regime; and consequently a starting point for a new appraisal on our part of the nature of the Soviet state (p. 68).

These lines prove how important the evolution of the buffer zone was for us and for the world workers' movement. Developments in the buffer zone also were of decisive importance for the Soviet Union.

We followed these developments passionately, meticulously. If you assemble everything that has been written in our ranks since 1946 on this question, it can be stated that we have never sinned in the domain of the concrete study of the events.

From the Third World Congress of the Fourth International, 1951 (reprinted from *Fourth International*, November–December 1951)

We may have committed errors in theoretical interpretation and in perspectives, but our study of the events was always very rigorous. No one ever contested the facts presented by the International as the basis of our discussions. All the discussions took these facts as their point of departure.

We must confine ourselves here to a reference for historical reasons only to the discussions we have had with those who had a different definition of the USSR than ours. These discussions with the theoreticians of "state capitalism" or of "bureaucratic collectivism" never had any bearing on the buffer zone, properly speaking; they were simply appendices to the discussion on the Russian question. Neither the supporters of the theory of "state capitalism" nor those of the theory of "bureaucratic collectivism" contested the facts assembled by the International. The facts had only a minor importance for them. Later on we will mention the discussions between comrades sharing our common theoretical basis.

Our movement took a position on the question of the buffer zone for the first time at the Preconference (March 1946) and at the 1st Plenum (June 1946). The resolution adopted by the Preconference noted:

> The introduction of a series of militarily and politically controlled countries into the economic sphere (of the USSR);
>
> The plundering and politically reactionary, conservative and capitulatory nature of the Soviet bureaucracy . . .
>
> The granting of governmental powers to the leaders of the Communist Parties regardless of their real strength;
>
> The elimination of oppositionist elements, the expropriation of foreign concessions, the acceleration of economic reforms by encouraging organs of dual power (committees of control of production, trade committees of poor peasants which carry out the agrarian reform).

This resolution declared itself in favor of the progressive reforms, for the right of the peoples to self-determination, for the free development of the workers' movement.

The 1st Plenum dealt especially with the occupation of numerous territories by the victor armies. The resolution said the following concerning the territories occupied by the Soviet armies:

> The Fourth International demands the withdrawal of all foreign armies, including the Soviet army, from all occupied territories.
>
> The Fourth International does not in any way abandon its slogan of the unconditional defense of the USSR. The Fourth International is likewise for the defense of the progressive measures which have been realized in the territories occupied by the Red Army . . .
>
> Wherever reactionary movements appear and, with the support of the imperialists, attempt to overthrow the more or less statified economy and to re-establish landed private property . . . we will oppose these movements and fight on the side of the Red Army for the defeat of the imperialists and their agents until the workers of these countries are strong enough to confront the bourgeois counterrevolution alone.
>
> In all the occupation zones our militants should defend our policy in such a manner so that it cannot be utilized against the Soviet Union to the advantage of imperialism.

We see then that in the first two positions, we clearly formulated our position on the defense of the USSR and the reforms carried out in the buffer zone against imperialism, and on the defense of the workers' movement of these countries against the bureaucracy, but that there is not a word on the nature of these states and their economies, nor on the tendencies of their development.

The first general theoretical position taken was formulated in the theses written by comrade Germain on "The USSR on the Morrow of the War" which appeared in the *International Bulletin,* September 1946. It was said that in a general way this study expressed the position of the International Secretariat, and it opened the discussion on the USSR, the buffer zone and Stalinism for the 2nd World Congress. Here is its essential part concerning the buffer zone question:

> Inherent in the system of production brought into being by the October Revolution

> is the tendency to break out of the frontiers of the USSR especially because the productive forces on a world scale cry out for collectivization. . . .
>
> Taking as our point of departure the tendency of the bureaucracy to 'structurally assimilate' the countries where it maintains its occupation over a whole period and which it wants to integrate into its economic system; taking likewise as our point of departure the impossibility of achieving this assimilation without the action of the working masses, it can be stated that the countries occupied by the Soviet bureaucracy can be divided into three zones:
>
> a) . . . all the territories incorporated into the USSR, there structural assimilation has been completed. . . .
>
> b) In Poland, in occupied Germany, in Yugoslavia and in Czechoslovakia, the beginnings of structural assimilation correspond to a very strong revolutionary impulsion or to an exceptional situation involving the physical disappearance of the propertied classes. . . . The nature of the economy and of the state remains bourgeois in these countries. However, the relationship of forces are such that for the moment the bourgeoisie is at the mercy of an action of the proletariat. It is only the bureaucracy's fear of the proletariat of these countries as well as of imperialism which keeps it from delivering a coup de grace to the native capitalists.
>
> c) In Finland, Austria, Hungary, Rumania and Bulgaria the state and the economy remain fundamentally bourgeois.

This long quotation needs no comment. In the discussion which occurred at the time, Marcoux, who had assembled a very important documentation on the question, examined the question in a static manner and even denied the existence of a tendency to structural assimilation; his point of view was rapidly outmoded by the march of events. On the other hand, comrade E.R. Frank, who was in agreement with the analysis, defined what was developing in the buffer zone as a tendency toward the establishment of a "state capitalism" based on a mixed economy (state capitalism and private property) and not toward the installation of a workers' state.*

At the 2nd World Congress (April 1948) which took place some weeks after the Prague coup, the discussion did not go beyond the positions previously taken by the International in 1946. In the Theses adopted by this Congress, the part dealing with the buffer zone describes the policy of the bureaucracy, there also verifying its dual character; it shows that due to the development of the international situation the bureaucracy despite itself found itself obliged to adopt a series of economic and political measures against the native bourgeoisie. It underscored the sharpening of the tendency toward total structural assimilation, but viewed this as possible only through a revolutionary mobilization of the masses in opposition to the bureaucracy. The Theses of the 2nd World Congress declared that the situation was transitory, but also that the economy of these countries remained capitalist and that the state remained a bourgeois state in its structure as well as in its function.

Politically the Congress confirmed our position of struggle against the restorationist tendencies and our support of the struggle of the masses for which it formulated a program of transitional demands. Finally, the state and the economy being characterized as capitalist, the Theses came out in favor of revolutionary defeatism in these countries in the event of war.

Viewed with hindsight, the discussion then was marking time as a result of the situation itself. It was necessary that the situation itself become further clarified for us to make further progress.

Some months after the 2nd World Congress, the split between the Yugoslav CP and the Cominform occurred. In the period which followed, important economic and also political developments began to occur in the buffer zone countries which transformed them considerably. All these events renewed the discussion and placed it on a new plane. On the other hand, the events in China were also to contribute in the clarification of our

* It should be pointed out, however, that when the discussion resumed at a later stage E.R. Frank was one of the first to make clear that capitalist property relations had been destroyed in the buffer zone, the process of "structural assimilation" having been completed.

thoughts on a whole series of problems, including those of the buffer zone.

### The 1949 resolution

The discussion led to the adoption of a resolution by the 7th Plenum in April 1949.

The 7th Plenum resolution described the developments which had occurred in the buffer zone since 1945, namely the period of agreements between Washington and the Kremlin, marked by agreements with what remained of the native bourgeoisie in the buffer zone countries, and then the period of "cold war" marked by a struggle against the economic and political positions of the native bourgeoisie, which was waged primarily with bureaucratic methods.

The 7th Plenum resolution concluded with a study of the theoretical significance of the evolution of the buffer zone countries. This latter part explains the transition regimes of the buffer zone countries as the resultant of the action of several factors: the decomposition of capitalism having attained a very advanced stage in these countries, the belatedness of the world revolution, and the role of the USSR as a workers' state but acting under the leadership of the bureaucracy with the methods peculiar to this caste. We have nothing essential to change on this point and that is why we have incorporated this part of the 7th Plenum resolution in the resolution submitted for adoption to the 3rd World Congress.

But a part of this same 7th Plenum resolution showed itself to be inadequate or ambiguous or false and the discussion immediately reopened. It was the part of the resolution dealing with the social nature of the buffer zone states which reactivated the debate. The resolution recognized that structural assimilation had reached a very advanced stage, it noted that the bourgeoisie was no longer in power as the ruling class. But it refused to say that the "leap" to workers' states had been made. The resolution considered these states as bourgeois states of a special type, something like "degenerated bourgeois states" although their structure—in the words of the resolution itself—was closer to that of the USSR than that of normal capitalist states. As a reason for this definition the resolution mentioned "the historic origins of the present situation and . . . the still indecisive social physiognomy" of the buffer zone countries. It indicated "the elimination of national frontiers between the buffer zone countries" as the "decisive and fundamental" factor for the completion of structural assimilation.

One year later, at the 8th Plenum, the discussion still continued in our ranks, and besides the adoption of a brief resolution on the class nature of Yugoslavia, two resolutions were submitted for a consultative vote of the Plenum, one by comrade Pablo, the other by comrade Germain, differing in the premises on which they based their definition of the Yugoslav state and in which the problem of the nature of the buffer zone countries was in fact inferred.

The developments which have occurred in the buffer zone since then have enabled us to overcome the differences which existed at the time and to evolve a very precise position, with an equally clear understanding of the reasons which caused the delay and the errors of our movement on the question of the buffer zone.

### The social nature of the buffer zone states

We believe that the buffer zone states are no longer capitalist states and that, like the USSR, they are fundamentally, i.e. in the domain of the relations of production and property, workers' states. The changes which were made in their economies, the extension of nationalization and planning to all spheres of the economy, fundamentally distinguish them from capitalist states.

What has happened in these countries *is not a quantitative increase* in nationalizations as has taken place in certain capitalist countries, *but a qualitative transformation of the economy.* It is not only heavy and light industry which is nationalized and planned but also the banks, all of transportation and all trade, foreign and domestic, wholesale as well as retail (in large part at least).

It is true that the land is not formally nationalized. This is not a negligible question, but it is not fundamental from the standpoint of a sociological characterization, in view of the considerable restrictions on the purchase and sale of land, and the introduction of collectivization on the countryside.

The relationships of production and property have been upset from top to bottom in these countries, and this transformation is continuing and involving spheres which have not as yet been affected (with the exception of agriculture with which we have already dealt). A return of these countries to a capitalist type structure will only be possible through a counterrevolution, which is obviously linked to the outcome of the coming war.

These are the fundamental changes of the economic structure which make us characterize these states as workers' states. There are, to be sure, important differences on the political and even on the economic plane among these states and between them and the USSR. That is not surprising. The evolution of varied human societies, among them workers' states, toward socialism cannot help but be affected by a whole series of factors. The march from capitalism to socialism will certainly give rise to very diverse social forms.

What is happening in the buffer zone countries is rather the obverse. The reactionary intervention of the Moscow bureaucracy tends to impose forms approximating those in the USSR upon these countries and also to Russify an important part of their state apparatuses for the purpose of assuring Kremlin control.

We are also witnessing on the plane of social relations in the buffer zone countries the imposition of a policy modeled on that of the Soviet bureaucracy which is directed towards the creation of an apparatus and socially privileged stratum in relation to the mass of the workers.

But all of these elements, which have a very great importance in determining our policy in these countries, are not decisive so far as the sociological characterization of these states is concerned.

Exception is made, in the resolution submitted to this Congress, in this sociological characterization of the buffer zone countries, for the Soviet zone in Austria which has not undergone any of these fundamental transformations.

### Deformed and degenerated workers' states

The resolution submitted to the Congress designates the buffer zone states as deformed workers' states. What do we mean by this designation?

We did not use the term degenerated workers' states because of the fact that this designation should only be applied (as in the case of the USSR) to a workers' state which was born in the revolutionary struggle of the masses and which subsequently deteriorated as a result of the bureaucratic seizure of power to the detriment of the working masses.

The buffer zone states are not the product of the revolutionary action of the masses but of the action of the bureaucracy, to which question we will return later. The defects they now have were present from the beginning. We do not mean "deformed" in the sense of workers' states marred by bureaucratic deformations as was the case with the USSR in the first years of its existence. In this context the word deformed means that these states have primarily the same fundamental defect as the USSR, i.e., the complete elimination of the proletariat, on the economic as well as the political plane, from the leadership of these countries.

In saying that we have been belated in characterizing these states as workers' states, we do not believe that we were wrong on this point in 1946 and at the time of the Second World Congress. We still believe that up to 1949 these states still retained a fundamentally capitalist structure, although it was considerably damaged from the capitalist point of view. The descriptions and analyses made by our movement up to 1949 were correct as a whole. We had correctly emphasized the principal tendencies of development. We were hesitant on the possibility of the realization of these tendencies under existing conditions or at least as we interpreted these conditions.

The transformation of bourgeois states (decayed) into deformed workers' states under the conditions it has occurred has raised a series of theoretical problems which should be dealt with.

For us, the norm in such a transformation is the revolutionary action of the masses, their armed struggle destroying the old apparatus of the bourgeois state and substituting a new state for it. The manner of the transformation in the buffer zone countries does not correspond to the norm. Essentially it was the result of the action of the bureaucracy of the USSR and its agents. Does this call for a revision of Marxism? We do not think so at all.

From what happened at the beginning of the Second World War and from the deductions Trotsky had drawn from these events, we were ready to grasp the tendency toward structural assimilation, to understand these phenomena as they occurred. But we hesitated in our theoretical generalizations. Why?

The bureaucracy is not a class, it has no fundamental role in history, it does not make history, on the contrary it seeks only to cheat history. But it has demonstrated an undeniable power, for reasons we well know, to deform and disfigure the march of the historic process. Stalinism falsifies past history, but it employs the same methods—and they are not without their consequences—on the present. We have seen Stalinism distort fundamental ideas in the minds of communist workers; we have seen it manipulate workers' organizations and their policy. The Kremlin bureaucracy, with all the material and political power it derives from the Soviet state, has been able to manipulate phenomena to the point of rendering them momentarily more or less unrecognizable, without however derailing the fundamental social forces and the laws of history. One of our primary weaknesses was that of not always being able to rapidly disentangle the profound nature of phenomena from the disfiguration they had suffered at the hands of the bureaucracy.

On the other hand, we ourselves did not exactly appreciate the conditions under which the bureaucracy had to operate. It is true that it acted in quite an empirical manner; in the beginning it did not dream of going beyond its agreements with imperialism. It merely wanted to convert the buffer zone states into zones of military protection and not into a belt of workers' states on the borders of the USSR. Molotov's declaration when Soviet troops entered the territory of a capitalist state for the first time, the theory of people's democracy (1st edition), was not contrived to deceive the bourgeoisie. The Kremlin bureaucracy had been obliged to go further than it intended. But we have only recently begun to appreciate more exactly the conditions under which the Kremlin acted. It is only approximately one year ago that we have begun to appreciate the grandeur of the revolutionary forces in all their scope let loose by the decomposition of capitalism. The discussion on the political report at this Congress has permitted an understanding of the full scope of these forces.

It is the decomposition of capitalism which has spoiled all the calculations of the bureaucracy as well as of imperialism in their search for a compromise which was also to include the buffer zone countries. We were especially cognizant of the bureaucratic character of the measures taken by the Kremlin but we were insufficiently appreciative of the forces which impelled the bureaucracy to reluctantly take the measures which in turn more and more barred the road to a compromise with imperialism and created a fundamentally different situation particularly in the buffer zone countries.

Among the causes of error on our part was the absolute juxtaposition of the action of the masses and that of the bureaucracy. We said: A workers' state is not the creation of bureaucratic action, but only of the revolutionary action of the masses. The bureaucracy, as we well know, never or almost never eliminates the action of the masses in its interventions; what it seeks to suppress is the action of the masses which it cannot rigorously control; but it is very well able to utilize the action of the masses which it can control in order to attain its own objectives at a given moment.

That was also true in the buffer zone countries. It placed the workers' movement there under its tutelage, it proceeded from purge to purge, it destroyed all initiative of the masses, all independent action to a considerable degree, but it nevertheless mobilized these masses in a form it completely controlled for the purpose of being able to proceed to the important changes it deemed necessary in the buffer zone countries. We did not believe that it could carry out an operation of such scope in the buffer zone countries without losing control of the mass movement.

Because we were not always capable of analyzing the deformative effects of bureaucratic action on the historic process, because we did not have an extremely precise estimation of the forces let loose by the decomposition of capitalism and because we did not always understand the utilization of the masses by the bureaucracy, we committed errors on the buffer zone question; and we became involved in a problem which was not the real one, because there was no real solution for it, namely that of the criterion which determines the moment when the "leap" takes place. We were not faced with a relatively normal process. History had gone through bureaucratic channels in these countries and the endeavor to apply rigorous norms there was not without its dangers.

It goes without saying that in recognizing the character of the bureaucratic action in the buffer zone countries we not only do not attribute any progressive character to it, not only do we continue to consider it as counterrevolutionary as a whole, but we underscore the limits of bureaucratic possibilities. They were brought to bear on bourgeois countries in full decomposition where social relations had already been very unstable before the war and where the bourgeoisie had been considerably undermined during the war.

It also goes without saying that the evolution of the buffer zone countries since 1945 does not provide the slightest justification for the theory of "people's democracy" (1st edition) which imitated the old social democratic revisionist conception of a possible gradual passage from capitalism to socialism. This theory has been a lamentable failure in Western European capitalist countries. In Eastern Europe, the bureaucratic intervention which was substituted for the revolutionary action of the masses had nothing whatever in common with gradual, organic evolution.

The buffer zone situation has also demonstrated several facts to us which lead to important theoretical or political conclusions.

The buffer zone situation demonstrated that the coming to power of Stalinist parties under bureaucratic conditions (contrary to those in Yugoslavia or China) had similar although less marked consequences on these parties. The contradictions of society were reflected in these parties with growing acuteness. The pressure of the masses made itself strongly felt in opposition to the demands of the Muscovite bureaucracy. The apparatus, even the leadership itself of these parties, is sensitive to this pressure. Thus far the tendencies expressing or reflecting this pressure have shown themselves extremely weak in face of the GPU apparatus, but one cannot exclude a different development in objectively different conditions.

Another very important point. The buffer zone experience has revealed—and even bourgeois observers have testified to this—that the working masses of these countries, although very hostile to the bureaucracy, are very attached to the transformations in the system even though they were achieved bureaucratically. Trotsky wrote in the definition of the USSR which he gave in *Revolution Betrayed* (p. 264): *"The social revolution betrayed by the government party still lives in the property relations and in the consciousness of the toilers."*

In the buffer zone countries as well, the social transformations not only live in the existing property relations but also in the consciousness of the toilers although these social relations occurred not in a revolutionary but in a bureaucratic way. That is a very important element for a proper appreciation of the buffer zone countries.

What we have learned on this point from the Ukrainian independence movement is also very significant. As a result of the division of the Ukraine before the Second World War, the Ukrainian nationalist movement in Poland had contributed in bringing independence tendencies into being in the Soviet Ukraine. But on the other hand, the difference in social system between these two sections of the Ukraine had led to the evolution of the Ukrainian nationalists in Poland toward the adoption of the social forms of property of the Soviet Ukraine. This is a phenomenon which should not be forgotten, especially in the case of present-day Germany.

### Policy toward the buffer zone countries

Our policy for the buffer zone countries, given the conclusion we have arrived at on their class nature and also the place they will have in the coming war, does not raise any moot problems. The discussion on the political resolution has clarified the problems posed by the buffer zone countries.

We are for the unconditional defense of these workers' states against imperialism in the war now being prepared. It is fundamentally the same problem as that of the defense of the USSR. We defend these states as working class conquests, regardless of the bureaucratic means which were used to bring them into being and regardless of the policy followed by their governments. Our defense of these states in no case, at no time, implies a limitation of our criticism of the policy followed by the governments of these states.

We have designated these states as deformed workers' states specifying that their deformation has been identical to that of the USSR principally in the expropriation of the proletariat from the administration of these states. It follows therefore that, as for the USSR, *our political program for these countries is that of political revolution* having as its aim the elimination of the bureaucracy from power and its resumption by the working masses. This point does not raise especially different problems from those of the USSR. Let us merely observe that there is not a native bureaucracy in these countries possessing a strength comparable to that of the Soviet bureaucracy; in truth, it is the Soviet bureaucracy which constitutes the principal prop, the principal strength of the native bureaucracies.

As in the case of the USSR, it is obvious that the defense of these countries does not exclude but on the contrary implies our support to movements of the worker and poor peasant masses against the bureaucracy. In the case of these countries, as in that of the national minorities in the USSR, we are also in favor of supporting mass movements for national independence from the yoke of the Soviet bureaucracy. In the buffer zone countries we are for the independence of these countries and their organization into a voluntarily organized federation.

All these points present no difficulties. They have long been the common property of our movement acquired on the question of the USSR in the past years by following step by step the evolution of the first workers' state. The only difference is that these countries suffer even more severely from their unequal relations with Moscow than do the nationalities of the USSR. Over the decades the national question has always been a very sensitive point in these countries. Finally the question of their federation has had a long tradition in the workers' movements of these countries, it having figured in the programs of socialist parties of these countries even before 1914.

In conclusion, we see that the buffer zone question has, in fact, been the extension of the Russian question which has so often been discussed in our movement, and not the point of departure for a new chapter in the history of the Soviet regime. But it is an extension which has taken its own peculiar course.

Our definition of the USSR, our comprehension of the dual role of the Soviet bureaucracy has permitted us to orient ourselves in a generally correct manner in the study of what has happened in the buffer zone countries and in understanding their fundamental tendencies. At bottom this was decisive.

But on the other hand, various inadequacies on our part have made us mark time, have led us into secondary problems and even into error. Today the situation has largely contributed in permitting us to overcome our weaknesses without great internal difficulties. It permits us to basically understand the buffer zone countries, their development, their contradictions.

We believe that the discussion based on the resolution presented by the International Secretariat will enable our movement to acquire all necessary clarity on this question and to seriously arm our militants for the political problems they will be faced with in the coming years.

**Summary speech by reporter**

After speeches by 15 delegates, the reporter made the following points:

The buffer zone was a relatively new phenomenon for which our only terms of reference were the occupation of territories by the Soviet army at the beginning of the Second World War. The term we employed in 1946, that of "structural assimilation," corresponded to our comprehension of this phenomenon at the time and of the perspectives of development we were then able to envisage. In light of what has occurred, a definition more closely approximating the phenomenon might possibly have been contrived. However, that did not appear necessary to us then, provided that more was not read into these words than was actually intended.

The words "structural assimilation" in the resolution do not mean that the buffer zone states have been incorporated in one or another form into the USSR or that their economies no longer have any independence in relation to that of the USSR. This term simply means that these states have fundamentally the same structure, the same fundamental relations of property and production as that of the first workers' state, the USSR. It is true, as the resolution points out, that the economic relations of these states with the USSR have been extended but that does not mean "structural assimilation" to us.

We live in a period of uninterrupted convulsions and that is why our theory should more than ever be a guide to action and not be transformed into rules which become abstractions when confronted with the reality. As is indicated in the report, one cannot apply the "norm," i.e. in this case, to demand to know the date on which the "leap" occurred. We will not repeat the explanation given in the resolution on this point. Let us only add that in a number of countries one would seek in vain for the "date" on which they passed over from feudalism to capitalism.

A comrade has mentioned the absence of nationalization on the land to prove the formation of new bourgeois strata in the country, thus creating dual power and an accumulation of dangers for these countries. We have pointed out in the report that the absence of nationalization of the land was an important question but not at all decisive for a characterization of the sociological nature of these countries.

It is true that tendencies toward the restoration of capitalism manifest themselves on the countryside in these countries because of their economic backwardness. But to proceed from there and to speak of new bourgeois strata is stretching the point too much; it is even less valid to speak of dual power. The facts do not support such statements. Tendencies are not yet a bourgeois class or dual power.

It is true that there are dangers to the non-capitalist structure of these states in possible developments on the countryside. That was the case with the USSR from the NEP up to 1928; although in this instance it must also be recognized that the danger was in nowise removed by nationalization of the land. The danger is also to be seen in Yugoslavia, which will be discussed on the next point of the agenda. But it is already possible to say that what makes these phenomena on the countryside dangerous in Yugoslavia is the considerable pressure now being brought to bear by imperialism on the country. The dominant pressure on the buffer zone countries at the present time comes from the opposite direction.

A comrade has raised the question of the application of the term "exploitation" to the Soviet bureaucracy. It is not a class, he says, and therefore its role in production is not that of exploitation in the Marxist sense of the term. Agreed. But if I am not mistaken the 2nd World Congress used the term "exploitation" for the mixed companies which the USSR had then imposed on the buffer zone countries. The Soviet state, in fact, played a capitalist role in these companies as is also the case with certain workers' organizations which engage in businesses associated with their general activity. The Soviet state acted as a capitalist in the case of the mixed companies and thus we have actually a case of exploitation.

The more complex question with which comrade Pablo has dealt is the one raised by several comrades on the completion of structural assimilation. We noted tendencies to structural assimilation beginning with 1945–46. From that time on, there existed potentially the possibilities of transformation which subsequently occurred. But its completion was the result of national and international factors.

The scope of nationalizations is not enough for an appreciation of the developments in the buffer zone countries. In 1946, there remained not only a capitalist economic structure, but the reconstructed states also had a capitalist political structure. With a different relationship of forces, another situation might have resulted in some of the buffer zone countries.

As a consequence of the "cold war," the Soviet bureaucracy was not only obliged to adopt a series of economic measures fundamentally transforming the economic structure of these states, but it also had to embark on a series of measures fundamentally transforming their political structure in order to align them with the structure of the USSR. The period in which these transformations occurred, bringing to completion the tendencies to structural assimilation which had existed from the beginning, dates clearly from the start of 1949, extends through that year and into 1950.

We also have to rectify what is erroneous in the draft document on the question of Albania. It is quite accurate that during the Second World War a development very much like that of Yugoslavia occurred in that country.

The question of the buffer zone has not only served to better arm us politically on the subject of Eastern Europe and of Asia but in general to help us better understand the period of transition from capitalism to socialism as we know it in its first stages.

# CLASS NATURE OF EASTERN EUROPE

The evolution of the European countries in the Soviet buffer zone since 1949 *has unfolded along the line of an accelerated integration of these countries into the economic and political orbit of the USSR.*

### Economic transformation

On the *economic* level this evolution has taken the fundamental line of a beginning of coordination and effective planning among their economies and with that of the USSR on the one hand, which has, on the other hand, considerably diminished their dependence upon the international capitalist economy and market.

Since 1949 we have observed the putting into effect of a series of long-range plans (five to six years) which, to the degree of their realization, detach these countries from a part of their ties with the external capitalist market and progressively fuse their economy into a whole which is more and more organically bound to the planned economy of the USSR.

These plans follow upon the actual statification of almost the whole of heavy and light industry, of foreign trade as well as important sectors of domestic trade, of transportation, and of a series of restrictive measures on property and on the private agricultural market, and following the generally successful execution of the first short-range plans (one to three years) which permitted the restoration of the economy to pre-war levels and the repairing of the destructions caused by the war.

From then on the statified economy has been governed by the necessities of the plan as in the USSR.

These developments have already effected a reversal of the previous tendency which marked the trade of these countries with the international capitalist market.

At present the trade of these countries amongst themselves and with the USSR accounts for more than half their foreign commerce and this trend is becoming more pronounced.

### New state apparatus created

On the *social* level, the state apparatuses of these countries are more and more coming to resemble that of the USSR with the creation, especially since the end of 1949, of bureaucratic People's Committees and by the more marked installation in all spheres of "reliable" elements who enjoy the confidence of the Soviet bureaucracy and are steadily replacing the old bourgeois elements.

The recruitment of these elements is now being stepped up from among the new workers' aristocracy which is favored by the regime by its methods of payment for labor and by the Stakhanovist movement, etc.

The state apparatus is thus "sovietized" both in its form as well as in its social composition by imitating the forms proper to the state apparatus of the USSR and by recruiting its functionaries among the new privileged sections. On the other hand, it is being "Russified" by placing in the most decisive posts of command in the civil, political and economic administration as well as in the police and in the army, elements directly manipulated by the Kremlin, and often actual Russian functionaries assuming the appropriate nationality.

### Outcome of political struggle

Finally, on the *political* level, if in a *historical sense* the fate of these countries has not yet been decided, the same cannot be said insofar as their *immediate fate* is concerned.

It is clear that the evolution of the international situation has not taken the line of a prolonged compromise between imperialism and the Soviet bureaucracy which could place the status of these countries in question, but rather on the contrary the line of accelerated preparation for war, wherein each seeks to consolidate its present sphere of influence.

The only possible exception is the case of the Soviet zone in Austria, which for the time being still remains an integral part of the Austrian state and on which a compromise involving the withdrawal of the occupation troops is not yet excluded.

On the other hand, the entire recent evolution of Eastern Germany, its structure and the execution of its five-year plan, and the deep-going modifications introduced into the state apparatus rather constitute an indication that Moscow, having lost hope of a general compromise particularly in regard to Germany, is passing over to the decisive integration of this area into the rest of the buffer zone. However, it is no less true that the political and economic structure of this area still remains quite different from that of the rest of the buffer zone.

On the other hand, the whole of the economic, social and political overturns which have occurred in the buffer zone have now acquired such a scope that the reintegration of these countries into the capitalist orbit can no longer be envisaged as possible by *"cold methods"* but only through a veritable capitalist counterrevolution (with the possible exception of Eastern Germany).

The example of the civil war now going on in Albania, by far the weakest link in the entire buffer zone, between the forces in the pay of native reaction and imperialism and the forces bound up with the present regime is conclusive on this point.

**End of intermediate status**

Taking into account all the modifications effected since 1949 in the economy as well as in the state apparatus of the buffer zone countries, within the framework of a new trend in the international situation, *the structural assimilation of these countries to the USSR must be considered as having now been essentially accomplished and these countries as having ceased to be basically capitalist countries.*

The taking into tow of all these countries by the Soviet bureaucracy after the last war, the influence and decisive control it exercised over them contained the *possibility* and even the *inevitability* of their structural assimilation to the USSR because of a certain internal and external relationship of forces between the Soviet bureaucracy, the native bourgeoisie, imperialism and the masses.

For a long period—approximately between 1945 and 1948—the Soviet bureaucracy maintained these countries in an *intermediate status* of varying degrees because it was not yet ready to consider its break with imperialism as final and because of the necessity imposed on it by its own nature of eliminating the native bourgeoisie by cold methods, without genuine revolutionary action by the masses over which it tried at the same time to exercise a rigorous control.

This intermediate status corresponded *sociologically* more and more to a regime of *dual power* both on the economic and the political planes, the economic structure remaining fundamentally capitalist. Beginning with 1949 this duality manifestly gave way to regimes which stabilized a structure essentially characterized by *property and productive relations* qualitatively assimilable to those of the USSR, that is to say, characteristic of an essentially *statified* and *planned* economy (except for the Soviet zone in Austria, where, because of the occupation, certain elements of dual power are noticeable).

Parallel with this process, the political power, which for a long time had been assumed by different combinations between the Stalinist leaderships and the representatives of the former bourgeois and petty-bourgeois parties, now passed exclusively into the hands of the Stalinists and was thus transformed in its form as well as in its social composition.

**Deformed workers' states**

The form of political power still remains marked by important differences from one country to another and in their entirety with that of the USSR, as is likewise the case so far as the form of political power in the capitalist system is concerned. But it is above all by virtue of their economic base, of the structure essentially common to all the countries of the buffer zone, characterized by new *production and property relations proper to a statified and planned economy, essentially like those of the USSR,* that we have to consider these states as now being *deformed workers' states.* These states have arisen not through the revolutionary action of the masses but through the military-bureaucratic action of the Soviet bureaucracy, thanks to exceptional circumstances created by the last war, and they are not administered directly by the proletariat but by a bureaucracy. The bureaucratic deformation of these states is of the same magnitude as that characterizing the USSR, the proletariat being totally deprived of political power just as in the USSR.

Consequently, as in the USSR, there is likewise posed as the task of the revolutionary vanguard of these countries a *political revolution* to overthrow the bureaucracy and open the road for the free development of socialism.

The further evolution of these countries and their immediate future are now bound to the fate of the conflict being prepared between imperialism on the one side and the USSR, these countries, China, the other colonial revolutions and the international working class movement on the other.

### Unconditional defense

Taking into account the class character of these countries and the reactionary war aims of imperialism, the Fourth International is neither neutral nor indifferent so far as the defense of these countries against imperialism is concerned. Just as in regard to the USSR, the Fourth International is for the *unconditional defense* of these countries against imperialism. It considers their structure of statified and planned economy as a conquest which must be safeguarded against imperialism, regardless of the policy followed by the governments vassalized to Stalinism in these countries.

That does not in any case signify the abandonment of our political opposition to these governments nor the subordination of our struggle for the world revolution to this defense. The contrary remains true. The Fourth International, within these countries, makes common cause with the proletarian and poor peasant masses who struggle against their exploitation and against the national oppression imposed by the domination of the Soviet bureaucracy, and it stands for the total independence of each of the countries in the buffer zone and for their organization into a freely agreed-upon federation.

### Examination of past position

In all the positions formerly taken on the question of the class nature of the countries of the Soviet buffer zone in Europe, the Fourth International pointed out the tendency of structural assimilation of these countries to the USSR and the *transitional state* in which these countries found themselves.

The Fourth International, on the other hand, indicated from the first that, under a certain correlation of forces between the Soviet bureaucracy, imperialism and the masses, the bureaucracy could even accomplish this assimilation.

During an entire period (1945–48) it was really impossible to conclude that such a relationship of forces favorable to the bureaucracy had been established and consequently to consider the fate of the countries in the buffer zone as decided for the entire immediate future.

Nevertheless it must be recognized that the International was kept from having a precise evaluation of the evolution in the buffer zone, of the speed and the scope of assimilation, because of a series of restrictive considerations like those set forth in the Second World Congress "Theses on the USSR and Stalinism" which asserted that "the genuine destruction of capitalism (in the buffer zone) is possible only through the revolutionary mobilization of the masses and the elimination of the special forms of exploitation introduced by the bureaucracy into these countries." On the other hand, in the Resolution of the Seventh Plenum of the International Executive Committee (May 1949) on "The Evolution of the Countries of the Buffer Zone," where there was more positively envisaged the possible perspective of a structural assimilation accomplished by the action of the Stalinist bureaucracy itself, it still insisted on "the abolition of frontiers which it could effect through the incorporation of certain or all of these countries into the USSR, or that it could accomplish through the constitution of a Balkan-Danubian federation formally independent of the USSR but a genuine unified framework for the planning of the economy."

### Process of bureaucratic change

It has turned out that the revolutionary action of the masses is not an *indispensable condition* needed by the bureaucracy to be able to destroy capitalism under exceptional and analogous conditions and in an international atmosphere like that of the "cold war." That does not mean that the bureaucracy completely deprives itself of mass action in destroying the bourgeoisie. It mobilized the masses *bureaucratically,* varying in scope from country to country and according to the given conditions, organizing them, for example, into "committees" of various kinds which played a certain role in disarming the bourgeoisie and in its economic and political expropriation. This bureaucratic mobilization of the masses, which is still proceeding in the struggle against the remnants of the possessing classes and especially against the well-to-do peasantry and the Catholic Church, is necessary because the bureaucracy is not an independent social force, a class, but supports itself partly upon the proletariat to struggle against the bourgeoisie even while lacing the masses at the same time into the straitjacket of its bureaucratic and police control.

It has turned out on the other hand that in such conditions and on the basis of an actual statification of the means of production, it is possible to initiate the process of a planned economy without formal incorporation into the USSR, without formal abolition of the frontiers and despite the special forms of exploitation that the bureaucracy still maintains in these countries which remain an ever-present obstacle to the planning and free development of their economy.

Regarding the theoretical significance of the evolution of the buffer zone and the conclusions that can be drawn concerning the role of Stalinism, the Fourth International still firmly stands on what has been said on this subject in the above-mentioned resolution of the Seventh Plenum of the IEC which is incorporated in the present resolution.

# THE YUGOSLAV REVOLUTION

1. The victorious proletarian revolution in Yugoslavia is fundamentally the product of two historic factors: the revolutionary upsurge of the toiling masses expressing itself in the movement of the armed partisans, and the specific policy followed by the Communist Party of Yugoslavia in the important turns of the objective revolutionary process.

*The movement of the masses of workers and poor peasants against the imperialist occupants,* in conditions of extreme sharpening of social contradictions, swelled the cadres fighting for national emancipation, broadened it into a struggle against the Yugoslav exploiters, took the first steps toward their expropriation and, in the very course of this struggle, destroyed the old state apparatus on the largest part of Yugoslav territory. *The specific policy of the CPY,* distinguishing itself from that of all the other Communist parties of Europe, primarily under the pressure of the masses, successively accepted, then took over the leadership in the destruction of the old bourgeois state apparatus; legalized, then generalized the construction of a new proletarian state apparatus; consolidated, then broadened the conquests of the proletarian revolution, by refusing to capitulate before the Soviet bureaucracy and by engaging in a resolute struggle against the bureaucratic deformations of the Yugoslav workers' state.

### Three stages of Yugoslav revolution

2. (a) The first decisive stage of the Yugoslav revolution was crossed on November 29, 1943 at the meeting of the second session of the AVNOJ (Yugoslav Anti-Fascist Council of National Liberation) at Jayce. On this occasion a provisional government was constituted which exercised its authority over all the territories occupied by the partisans which soon embraced the major part of Yugoslavia. The constitution of this government, basing itself on *people's committees* of national liberation, which came into existence in 1941, signified that the dual power, which had existed in Yugoslavia from the beginning of the partisan insurrection, was being overcome. From this time on, there can be no further question of the existence of a centralized bourgeois state apparatus in Yugoslavia; there remained only the ruins of bourgeois power, just as the successive measures of expropriation and confiscation left only the ruins of bourgeois property. The new centralized state apparatus, based on the people's committees, which the AVNOJ began to construct, was a preponderantly proletarian state apparatus. The CPY having in fact conquered power in the liberated territories, this part of Yugoslavia ceased to be a bourgeois state; under a workers' and peasants' government it advanced toward the final accomplishment of the proletarian revolution.

(b) The second decisive stage of the Yugoslav revolution was crossed in October 1945 *with the withdrawal of the two last bourgeois ministers from the central provisional government.* The very constitution of this government in 1944 was only an episode in the unfolding of the Yugoslav revolution and was imposed by the joint pressure of imperialism and the Soviet bureaucracy. While retarding the complete victory of the proletarian revolution, this episode, however, did not interrupt its progress. During the very period of the coalition government, the new state apparatus based on the people's committees was extended over the whole Yugoslav territory. During this period all the remnants of bourgeois political power were eliminated. The withdrawal of the two bourgeois ministers from the central government was only the final expression of the fact that the bourgeoisie as a class had lost power and that the new state apparatus was of a socially different character than that of prewar Yugoslavia. *Beginning with this time, the transition between the workers' and peasants' government and the dictatorship of the proletariat was being completed and Yugoslavia became a workers' state.* That was manifested by the fact that the conquests of the Yugoslav proletarian revolution were generalized and legally consolidated in 1945–46 by the law on the people's committees, the law of nationalization of the means of industrial production, the mines and the banks and by the law on the confiscation of property, the law on agrarian reform and the annulment of peasant debts, etc.

(c) The third decisive stage of the Yugoslav revolution was crossed on June 28, 1948 by the split which occurred between the Kremlin and the CPY. After the consolidation of the conquests of the Yugoslav revolution, the CPY proceeded to their extension by the nationalization of wholesale trade and a considerable part of retail trade; the establishment of a monopoly of foreign trade; the beginning of the collectivization of agriculture and the five-year plan of industrialization and electrification of the country. At the same time bureaucratic deformations of the proletarian power developed in Yugoslavia both as a result of the backward character of the country and of the Stalinist policy of the leadership of the CPY, imitating the institutions of the bureaucratized USSR. *The split between the Kremlin and the CPY, the expression of the refusal of the CPY to subordinate the interests of the Yugoslav revolution to those of the Soviet bureaucracy, opened the road to the struggle against these bureaucratic deformations.* The principal measures taken within the framework of this struggle were: the constitution of workers' councils and the beginning of workers' management of the enterprises; the democratization of the cooperatives; the abolition of the privileges of the functionaries of the party and the state; the decentralization of the directing apparatus of the economy; the beginning of the democratization of cultural and ideological life, etc.

### Permanent revolution confirmed

3. The dynamics of the Yugoslav revolution confirms the theory of the permanent revolution on all points:

(a) It confirms the point that the struggle of the toiling masses for national liberation against imperialism can only be victorious if it is transmuted into a proletarian revolution. This transmutation in Yugoslavia was not due to particular or conjunctural factors but constituted the application of the general strategy formulated by the Fourth International for all countries occupied by imperialism in Europe during the Second World War. If this strategy was successfully applied only in Yugoslavia, that is due to the specific character of the CPY which headed the movement of the masses.

(b) It confirms the point that a backward country can resolve the historic tasks of the bourgeois revolution (solution of the agrarian question, elimination of semifeudal survivals in the state power, conquest of genuine national independence, etc.) only by the conquest of power by the proletariat which, in such conditions, finds itself compelled to grapple simultaneously with the solution of the historic tasks of the proletarian revolution.

(c) It confirms the point that the development and broadening of proletarian democracy after the consolidation of proletarian power is both possible and necessary to effectively combat the antisocialist and bureaucratic tendencies which exist and develop in the workers' state. In this, it represents a confirmation and a *positive* historical justification of the entire struggle of Leon Trotsky and the Left Opposition in the USSR between 1923 and 1927, just as the degeneration of the USSR constituted a justification along *negative lines.*

(d) It confirms the point that a victorious proletarian revolution in a backward country, in the midst of a hostile world, necessarily develops through growing difficulties and contradictions which are reflected in economic crises and successive social tensions within the workers' state. Only an international extension of the revolution and the aid given to the Yugoslav revolution by the victorious proletariat of several advanced countries can assure a real and harmonious solution of the problems posed by industrialization and the voluntary collectivization of agriculture.

At the same time the dynamics of the Yugoslav revolution confirms the analysis made by the Fourth International of the questions of the USSR and of Stalinism. It confirms the character of the Stalinist parties as degenerated workers' parties, an indispensable explanation in understanding the new course taken by the Yugoslav revolution since the break between the CPY and the Kremlin. It especially confirms the fundamental thesis of the Trotskyist movement which maintains that Stalinism is a phenomenon characteristic of a period of ebb in the revolutionary struggles of the masses, and that it can be overcome only by a new rise of revolutionary struggles. In Yugoslavia, the first country where the proletariat took power since the degeneration of the USSR, Stalinism no longer exists today as an effective factor in the workers' movement, which however does not exclude its possible reemergence under certain conditions.

## Relationship of class forces internally

4. *The perspectives of the Yugoslav revolution are fundamentally determined by the relationship of forces between the classes on the national and international arenas.*

In Yugoslavia, the workers' state is confronted with growing pressure from the peasant proprietors who seek to pass from simple commodity production to capitalist accumulation by means of the private appropriation of the means of production. This tendency develops automatically and necessarily on the basis of the present economic and technical development of the country and coincides with the tendency of the kulaks to effect their fusion with the international capitalist market.

At present this is being held in check as follows:

(a) By the slow modification of the relationship of social forces resulting from the industrialization of the country, from the numerical increase of the proletariat, of its cohesion, its political consciousness and its growing cultural progress, thanks to the beginning of the development of proletarian democracy, etc.

(b) By the differentiation within the peasantry itself, resulting from the support given by the workers' state to the poor peasants and to the development of agricultural cooperatives.

(c) By measures of coercion taken by the workers' state hindering the development of this automatic economic process: prohibition of the sale and purchase of land over 30 hectares; dual price sector; progressive quotas of forced deliveries of farm products (tax in kind); etc.

Nevertheless, so long as the industrial production of objects of consumption does not assure to the peasants a real growing return parallel with the growth of agricultural production, and so long as the mechanization of agriculture is not able to create a healthy economic base for the collectivization of agriculture, industrialization will be carried on amidst the hostility and resistance of a section of the peasantry. Under these conditions only the conscious participation of the proletariat in the exercise of power can protect the conquests of the revolution in the immediate period. Only a considerable extension of the present measures of democratization and of the struggle against bureaucratism can assure the conscious support of the proletarian masses for the workers' state.

However, the measures of democratization introduced in 1950 have only very slowly altered the attitude of the industrial proletariat, as a result of its justified past distrust toward this course of the CPY, as a result of the pressure of famine and poverty upon the workers and as a result of unfavorable objective conditions for a broad revolutionary mobilization of the masses. The needs of the industrial proletariat also began to come into conflict with the inherent logic of the rightward course and the official ideology of the government and the CPY. Because of this fact, the relationship of forces between the classes within Yugoslavia have begun to alter beginning with 1951 to the disadvantage of the proletariat. The workers' state has been obliged to make a series of concessions to the class enemy consisting notably of the following:

(a) The removal of controls from prices and trade, permitting an accelerated private accumulation on the part of rich peasants and tradesmen-speculators.

(b) The halting of agrarian collectivization and the permission granted to the peasantry to withdraw from certain types of agricultural cooperatives.

(c) The decentralization of foreign trade which threatens to rapidly undermine the state monopoly of foreign trade.

## Under imperialist and Kremlin pressure

5. On the international plane, a growing pressure is being brought to bear upon the Yugoslav

revolution by its two mortal enemies—world imperialism and the Soviet bureaucracy:

(a) World imperialism seeks to destroy the conquests of the Yugoslav revolution, the regime of the dictatorship of the proletariat and the collectivized property in the means of production in industry and in the mines. It reckons on succeeding by stages in this game: first by the utilization of political and economic pressure, then by an open or camouflaged armed intervention. Its objectives at the present stage are: the inclusion of Yugoslavia in the imperialist diplomatic front and in its Mediterranean military alignments. With that beginning, it seeks to obtain at a later stage the right to supervise Yugoslav economy, the right of investment in the mines and industry, the legalization of the bourgeois and petty-bourgeois political parties, the virtual destruction of the monopoly of foreign trade, etc.

(b) The Soviet bureaucracy seeks by all means to bring about the destruction of a regime of the dictatorship of the proletariat independent of the Kremlin, a mortal threat to the influence of Stalinism over the international workers' movement, and in the long run also to the power of the bureaucracy in Eastern Europe and in the USSR itself. The destruction by imperialism of the conquests of the Yugoslav proletarian revolution represents a lesser evil to the Kremlin than the independent development of proletarian Yugoslavia. Up to now, the entire policy of the Kremlin toward Yugoslavia (economic blockade, provocative military demonstrations, propaganda campaigns, etc.) is aimed at forcing this country into the imperialist camp. This policy, however, is only a preparation for another stage of the counterrevolutionary strategy of Stalinism toward Yugoslavia which would consist in an attempt to include Yugoslavia in the sphere of influence of the Soviet bureaucracy by means of military intervention.

In the long run, this hostile, twofold pressure brought to bear on the Yugoslav revolution can only be successfully counteracted by the conscious support of the world proletariat and the international victory of the socialist revolution. For the present, the situation of unstable equilibrium between imperialism and the Soviet bureaucracy accords a certain respite to the Yugoslav revolution. But this respite occurs, especially since the outbreak of the war in Korea, within the framework of an *increased parallel pressure* brought to bear upon Yugoslavia, a pressure which is not neutralized by a sufficiently extensive international proletarian action for the aid of Yugoslavia. In these conditions the Yugoslav state has found itself constrained to make a series of concessions to its enemies on the international plane. It has led to an opportunist deviation in its foreign policy and especially that of the CPY (idealization of the UN, neutralism, petty-bourgeois concept of aggression, pacifist conception of class collaboration in the struggle against war, etc.).

*Without a radical alteration of the relationship of forces between the classes on the international arena, this tendency threatens to deepen and to hurtle the Yugoslav revolution to its doom. The contradiction between the progressive evolution of the Yugoslav state itself in 1950 and the rightward evolution of its foreign policy which, at the present stage, is the expression of the crisis of isolation of the Yugoslav revolution, will find a solution at a later stage in one of two ways: either the Yugoslav socialist revolution will fuse with the revolutionary movement and with the international revolution, or international concessions to imperialism will be followed by concessions within Yugoslavia itself.*

But despite the right deviation of its foreign policy and despite all the concessions which it has already been obliged to make to the class enemy in Yugoslavia itself, the leadership of the CPY and of the Yugoslav workers' state cannot itself peacefully abolish the material bases of this state without destroying itself. American imperialism and the rich peasantry of Yugoslavia have only a transitory interest in dealings with the CPY and in wresting concessions from it; their fundamental interest requires the destruction of the workers' state and the return to power of the bourgeois politicians who are already raising their heads. That is why the policy of the CPY in the period ahead, *a period of sharpened social struggles in Yugoslavia,* will be characterized by its *vacillating centrist* character which can abruptly change its rightward course to an adventurist struggle against the kulaks and an attempt to keep the power by all means. Fundamentally, the question of whether the CPY will be obliged to deepen workers' democracy, a step which cannot fail to have its repercussions on the foreign policy of the party, will depend on the degree of the *real activity* of the Yugoslav proletariat in the workers' councils and the people's committees, or whether in the absence of a real mobilization of the masses, the regime will take more and more bureaucratic forms.

### Character of Yugoslav Communist Party

6. It is impossible to determine the dynamics and the perspectives of the Yugoslav revolution without at the same time defining the character of the CPY. *If Stalinism can be defined as the subordination of the interests of the workers of every country to those of the Soviet bureaucracy, the CPY, beginning with 1941, outlined an orientation which was to lead to the break of 1948 and, because of this fact, it ceased to be a Stalinist party in the full meaning of the word.* The difference in orientation between the CPY and that followed by the other CPs of Europe was effected in the first place under the pressure of the masses. But that does not suffice to explain the evolution of Yugoslavia. In other countries, where the revolutionary upsurge, at least at the beginning, was as powerful as in Yugoslavia (Spain 1936, Greece 1944), the CPs took a diametrically opposite course to that of the CPY. The difference in orientation between the CPY and those of the other CPs of Europe could result only from an *interaction* between the revolutionary pressure of the masses and the changes of strategic conceptions which they produced in the leadership of the CPY under favorable conditions, to which should be added the absence of a Kremlin control apparatus operating on the scene.

In the first stage, these changes expressed themselves by an attempt of the leadership of the CPY to *conciliate* the interests of the Yugoslav revolution with those of the Soviet bureaucracy (1941 to early 1948). For this reason, while remaining within the international framework of Stalinist policy and while publicly and unreservedly accepting the internal and external policy of the Soviet bureaucracy, the CPY nevertheless differentiated itself at the time from Stalinist policy on the following points:

(a) The creation, 1941, of "people's committees of national liberation" and of "proletarian brigades" in the partisan movement.

(b) The refusal to collaborate, in 1942, with Mikhailovich's Chetniks and with the bourgeois government-in-exile.

(c) The orientation, in 1943, towards the actual seizure of power by the CPY and the constitution of an apparatus of a new state, of a proletarian type.

(d) Elimination, in 1945, despite the agreements of "the Big Three," of the last vestiges of bourgeois power in the country and the completion of the proletarian revolution.

(e) The pursuit of a foreign policy and an economic orientation more independent from the Kremlin than that of the other countries of the buffer zone.

The accumulation of all these actions, accompanied by an initial private criticism of the whole of Stalinist policy (notably: criticism of the more exorbitant privileges of the top functionaries of the USSR; criticism of the relations of economic plunder imposed on the buffer zone countries by the bureaucracy; criticism of the policy of the French, Italian and Greek CPs, at the time of the "liberation," etc.), led the Kremlin to the *preventive split* with the CPY. *This split was inevitable because of the irreconcilability of interests between the Yugoslav revolution and the Soviet bureaucracy.*

Beginning with this split there opened a second stage of differentiation between the CPY and Stalinism. Progressing in a purely empirical fashion, the CPY has successively emphasized:

(a) The subordination of the international communist movement to the interests of the Kremlin and the defeats to the workers' movements of several countries caused by this subordination.

(b) The total political, economic, military, cultural grip of the Soviet bureaucracy on the countries of the buffer zone and its horrible consequences for the toiling masses of these countries.

(c) The fundamental orientation of the Soviet bureaucracy toward a division of the world through the establishment of a *modus vivendi* with imperialism and the utilization of the workers' movement as barter for this purpose.

(d) The degeneration of the USSR as a result of the isolation of the first workers' state and of its backward character and the formation of a privileged bureaucratic caste which has usurped all power in the USSR.

(e) The danger of bureaucratism in every proletarian revolution, a danger which can be combated only by increasing proletarian democracy.

(f) The necessity of reconstructing the workers' movement in several countries.

### Centrist policy and ideology

Beginning with this time, the CPY ceased to be a semi-Stalinist party and evolved as a centrist party, carried to power by the revolutionary masses. On the other hand it is characterized by right-opportunist deviations, the most important being:

(a) The empirical character of its ideological development which has still not grasped the full Leninist conception of the nature of our epoch.

(b) The pragmatic and unprincipled character of the foreign policy of the CPY, tending to justify the diplomatic maneuvers of the Yugoslav state.

(c) The underestimation of the international workers' movement and the lack of understanding of the theory of the permanent revolution as a whole.

(d) The absence of the right to form tendencies within the CPY.

(e) An opportunist conception of the construction of revolutionary parties in the world (generalization of the Yugoslav experience, underestimation of the importance of program, etc.).

(f) Since the right turn in Yugoslav foreign policy, the pragmatic elaboration of a theory of "State Capitalism" on the USSR joined to neo-reformist conceptions on "new forms" of capitalism, etc.

Only a modification of the international relationship of forces between the classes, a rise of the world revolutionary movement, assistance and fraternal criticism from this movement and a growing understanding on the part of the leaders and cadres of the CPY, will enable it to avoid crystallizing on false positions which would lead to the liquidation of the progressive effects of the Yugoslav affair.

Already, the positions taken as a result of the war in Korea have in part vitiated the effects of the Yugoslav affair on the international crisis of Stalinism; in these conditions and in the absence of a sufficiently strong revolutionary international leadership, it is not excluded that Stalinism can regain a foothold in the ranks of the CPY.

In this connection, the positions and the attitude the CPY takes toward Trotskyism—whether openly or by attempting to ignore it—acquires considerable political importance. What is involved is not merely a historic rectification of the past; *it is the test of whether a workers' current which has emerged from Stalinism has succeeded in linking itself with the tradition and program of Bolshevism,* and thereby in definitively and decisively surmounting Stalinism.

### Tasks of the Fourth International

7. The tasks of the Fourth International toward the Yugoslav revolution are established within the framework of its general strategy, conforming to this analysis of the character of the Yugoslav state and the CPY:

(a) *The Fourth International unconditionally defends the conquests of the Yugoslav revolution against world imperialism and against the Soviet bureaucracy.* It conceives of this defense both as a strategic task—the junction of the international revolution with the Yugoslav revolution—and as an immediate tactical task: mobilization of the international revolutionary vanguard and of the proletarian masses of all countries for concrete actions in defense of the conquests of the Yugoslav proletarian revolution.

This defense cannot enter into collision with the interests of the world revolution of which the conquests of October form part. The Fourth International will likewise assure the defense against any attempt by internal forces to utilize Yugoslavia against the interests of the world revolution.

(b) In the event of war by the Soviet bureaucracy against Yugoslavia, the Fourth International will be *for the defense of Yugoslavia against the counterrevolutionary action of the Kremlin.* This policy, based on the interests of the world revolution, will be pursued regardless of all material aid Yugoslavia may eventually receive from capitalist countries. In event of an extension of the conflict this position will be reexamined in each specific case.

(c) The Fourth International will attempt to involve the CPY in *united front* actions for specific objectives. Each of these actions presupposes our principled agreement regarding the objective to be attained, and cannot in any case eliminate the right of the international revolutionary movement to criticize the policy of the Yugoslav government and the CPY. The practical possibility of realizing such actions is extremely limited because of the present rightward course of the CPY.

(d) The Fourth International believes that one of its principal contributions to the consolidation of the conquests of the Yugoslav revolution consists in a frank and uncompromising criticism of all the political errors and opportunist deviations on the part of the CPY. These criticisms should take as their point of departure the concrete experiences of the international workers' movement which must be communicated to the CPY as well as of the peculiar experience of the Yugoslav revolution; they should tend to impel the Yugoslav communists to replace their present opportunist leadership by a revolutionary leadership which in practice applies a policy corresponding both to the interests of the international proletariat and the safeguarding of the Yugoslav revolution: a break with the imperialist diplomatic front, a halting to the economic and political concessions to imperialism, an effective mobilization of the workers and poor peasants against the kulaks and speculators, a deepening of workers' democracy, freedom of discussion, assembly and press for all the currents of the workers' movement basing themselves on proletarian power in Yugoslavia, support to the international workers' movement and genuine support to a real international revolutionary regroupment.

### A critique of past positions

8. It is the duty of the Fourth International to critically reexamine, in the light of the events which have occurred since 1948, its past analysis of the Yugoslav revolution and the dynamics of this revolution which events have placed in a new light.

From 1942 on, the Fourth International had in general correctly estimated the movement of the Yugoslav partisans and the civil war which unfolded as a consequence. This analysis continued along correct lines up to the beginning of 1946. From that time and until June 28, 1948, the International committed serious errors of evaluation regarding the Yugoslav revolution; they consisted notably in an identification of the Yugoslav developments with those of the other buffer zone countries; in confounding the CPY with the Stalinist parties in the buffer states; in the erroneous hypothesis that the revolutionary movement of the masses had been arrested by the CPY and that the new centralized state apparatus constructed by the CPY was a bourgeois state apparatus in its structure, despite the elimination of the bourgeoisie from the political and economic life of the country which had been noted by the International.

*After the break of the Kremlin with the CPY, the Fourth International was the only tendency of the international workers' movement to immediately understand the progressive significance and the historic import of this event and to undertake an international campaign for the defense of Yugoslavia; it linked the analysis it made of the causes of the break with the analysis it had made before 1946 of the depth of the revolutionary mass movement in Yugoslavia. The campaign for the defense of Yugoslavia was, however, partly hindered by the delay of the International in recognizing the character of Yugoslavia as a workers' state.* This delay was due fundamentally to a false appraisal of the nature of the centralized state apparatus set up in Yugoslavia in 1945.

These various errors of evaluation were caused by:

(a) The absence of precise information on Yugoslav events and institutions beginning with the years 1945–46.

(b) The absence of all public differentiation by the CPY in relation to the Soviet bureaucracy and to Stalinism before June 28, 1948.

(c) The fact that the correct general analysis of the primarily counterrevolutionary role of the Soviet bureaucracy in the buffer zone led the International to identify *a priori,* without separate analysis of each case, the policy of the CPs with that of the bureaucracy (which was not only wrong for Yugoslavia, but also for China).

The lesson to be drawn from these errors of evaluation is the imperious necessity of *concrete and precise* analyses of the national peculiarities in the development of the workers' movement of every country. However important in our epoch are the laws of development for sectors of the world or for the entire world, these laws can never *be substituted* for the particular analysis of each country in the determination of a correct day-to-day revolutionary policy.

The rapidity and the unanimity with which the Fourth International was able, on the morrow of June 28, 1948, to make a turn for the defense of Yugoslavia, as well as the concrete manner it has followed and appraised the evolution of the CPY since then, prove that these errors of evaluation were not at all due to an erroneous general conception, but rather occurred despite the correct evaluation made by the Fourth International of the nature of Stalinism and its dialectical relationships with the mass movement. It is only in the light of this appraisal that the Yugoslav revolution becomes comprehensible and assumes its full significance as an important stage in the world crisis of Stalinism.

# CAPITALIST CRISIS AND THE FIGHT FOR WORKERS POWER

*New Expanded Edition!*

## Cosmetics, Fashion, and the Exploitation of Women

MARY-ALICE WATERS
JOSEPH HANSEN
EVELYN REED

"Norms of beauty and fashion are inseparable from the class struggle." That's the title of the opening chapter of this timely new edition of a lively 1950s debate in the *Militant*, a socialist newsweekly. How cosmetics and fashion monopolies rake in profits from social insecurities of women and adolescents. Why women's integration into the workforce and unions is a major advance in the fight for emancipation. A Marxist classic on the origins of women's oppression and the working-class road forward. $15. Also in Spanish, French, Farsi, Greek.

## The Truth About Yugoslavia

### Why Working People Should Oppose Intervention

GEORGE FYSON
ARGIRIS MALAPANIS
JONATHAN SILBERMAN

How the US rulers, in collaboration with their NATO allies and rivals, used deadly bombs and cruise missiles to finish off the Yugoslav Revolution's conquest of national unification. In the process, Washington reinforced its place as the dominant "European" military power. $7. Also in Greek.

## The Communist Manifesto

KARL MARX AND FREDERICK ENGELS

Communism, say the founding leaders of the revolutionary workers movement, is not a set of ideas or preconceived "principles" but workers' line of march to power. It springs from a "movement going on under our very eyes." $5. Also in Spanish, French, Farsi, Arabic.

## The Jewish Question

### A Marxist Interpretation

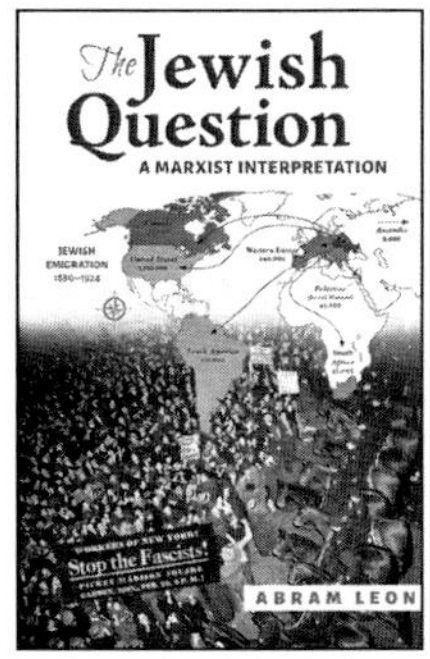


ABRAM LEON

The battle against reactionary forces aiming to exterminate the Jews remains central to world politics, as shown by the genocidal October 2023 pogrom in Israel. Why is Jew-hatred still raising its ugly head? What are its class roots? Why, as Abram Leon explains, is there no solution "independent of the world proletarian revolution"? Revised translation, new introduction, 40 pages of illustrations and maps. $17. Also in Spanish, French, Greek.

## Teamster Rebellion

FARRELL DOBBS

The 1934 strikes that won union recognition for truckers and warehouse workers in Minneapolis and helped pave the way for the working-class social movement that built the industrial unions. The first of four volumes by a central leader of these battles and of the Socialist Workers Party. $16. Also in Spanish, French, Farsi, Greek.

## U.S. Imperialism Has Lost the Cold War

JACK BARNES

The collapse of regimes across Eastern Europe and the USSR claiming to be communist did not mean workers and farmers there had been crushed. In today's sharpening class conflicts and wars, these toilers are joining working people the world over in the class struggle against capitalist exploitation. In *New International* no. 11. $14. Also in Spanish, French, Farsi, Greek.

## The Clintons' Anti-Working-Class Record

### Why Washington Fears Working People

JACK BARNES

What working people need to know about the profit-driven course of Democrats and Republicans alike over the last three decades. And the political awakening of workers seeking to understand and resist the capitalist rulers' assaults. $10. Also in Spanish, French, Farsi, Greek.

# WORKING-CLASS LEADERSHIP AND THE SOCIALIST REVOLUTION

*New!*

## Revolution and the Road to Peace in Colombia

### The Example of the Cuban Revolution

FIDEL CASTRO

"No crime can be committed in the name of revolution," Fidel Castro declares, drawing from the example set by working people of Cuba as they took state power out of the hands of its capitalist rulers. In 2008, as part of efforts to end six decades of armed conflict in Colombia, he shared the exemplary record of Cuba's revolutionary struggle with the Revolutionary Armed Forces of Colombia (FARC) and the world. $10. Also in Spanish.

## Lenin's Final Fight

### Speeches and Writings, 1922–23

V.I. LENIN

In 1922 and 1923, V.I. Lenin, central leader of the world's first socialist revolution, waged what was to be his last political battle—one that was lost after his death. At stake was whether that revolutionary government and the world communist movement it led would remain on the revolutionary proletarian course that brought workers and peasants to power in Russia in 1917. $17. Also in Spanish, Farsi, Greek.

## Malcolm X Talks to Young People

"The young generation of whites, Blacks, browns, whatever else—you're living at a time of revolution," said Malcolm in 1964. "And I for one will join with anyone, I don't care what color you are, as long as you want to change this miserable condition that exists on this earth." Four talks and an interview in the last months of Malcolm's life. $12. Also in Spanish, French, Farsi, Greek.

## Che Guevara on Economics and Politics in the Transition to Socialism

CARLOS TABLADA

It's essential for working people to win state power, said Ernesto Che Guevara. "Then there's the second stage, maybe more difficult than the first"—the transition from dog-eat-dog capitalism to socialism. A new edition with substantially expanded selections from Guevara's writings. $17. Also in Spanish.

## The Revolution Betrayed

### What Is the Soviet Union and Where Is It Going?

LEON TROTSKY

In 1917 workers and peasants of Russia were the motor force of one of the deepest revolutions in history. Yet within ten years a political counterrevolution by a privileged social layer, whose chief spokesperson was Joseph Stalin, was being consolidated. The classic study of the Soviet workers state and its degeneration. $17. Also in Spanish, Farsi, Greek.

## Opening Guns of World War III: Washington's Assault on Iraq

JACK BARNES

The murderous assault on Iraq in 1990–91 heralded increasingly sharp conflicts among imperialist powers, growing instability of capitalism, and more wars. Also includes:

**1945: When US Troops Said 'No!'**
by Mary-Alice Waters

**Lessons from the Iran-Iraq War**
by Samad Sharif

In *New International* no. 7. $14. Also in Spanish, French, Farsi.

# EXPAND YOUR REVOLUTIONARY LIBRARY

## Labor, Nature, and the Evolution of Humanity

### The Long View of History

FREDERICK ENGELS
KARL MARX
GEORGE NOVACK
MARY-ALICE WATERS

Without understanding that social labor, transforming nature, has driven humanity's evolution for millions of years, working people are unable to see beyond the capitalist epoch of class exploitation that warps all human relations, ideas, and values. $12. Also in Spanish and French.

## Thomas Sankara Speaks

### The Burkina Faso Revolution, 1983–87

Under Sankara's guidance, Burkina Faso's revolutionary government led peasants, workers, women, and youth to expand literacy; to sink wells, plant trees, erect housing; to combat women's oppression; to carry out land reform; to join others worldwide to free themselves from the imperialist yoke. $20. Also in French.

## Cuba and the Coming American Revolution

JACK BARNES

This is a book about the example set by the Cuban people that socialist revolution is not only necessary—it can be made. A book about the struggles of workers and other exploited producers in the imperialist heartland, and the youth attracted to them. About the class struggle in the US, where the revolutionary capacities of working people are as utterly discounted by the ruling powers as were those of the Cuban toilers. $10. Also in Spanish, French, Farsi.

## Imperialism's March Toward Fascism and War

JACK BARNES

"There will be new Hitlers, new Mussolinis. That is inevitable. What is not inevitable is that they will triumph. The working-class vanguard will organize our class to fight back against the devastating toll we are made to pay for the capitalist crisis. The future of humanity will be decided in the contest between these contending class forces." *In New International* no. 10. $14. Also in Spanish, French, Farsi, Greek.

## To See the Dawn

### Baku, 1920—First Congress of the Peoples of the East

How can peasants and workers in the colonial world achieve freedom from imperialist exploitation? By what means can working people overcome divisions incited by their national ruling classes and act together for their common class interests? These questions were addressed by 2,000 delegates to the 1920 Congress of the Peoples of the East. $17

## Essential Works of Lenin

Contains *What Is to Be Done?* as well as *State and Revolution* and *Imperialism: The Highest Stage of Capitalism.* $17

## Women in Cuba: The Making of a Revolution Within the Revolution

VILMA ESPÍN
ASELA DE LOS SANTOS
YOLANDA FERRER

The integration of women in the ranks and leadership of the Cuban Revolution was intertwined with the proletarian course led by Fidel Castro from the start. This is the story of that revolution and how it transformed the women and men who made it. $17. Also in Spanish, Farsi, Greek.